Jacob's Well Publishing
45 Buford Lane
Poplarville, Ms 39470
www.jacobswellrecoverycenter.com

Scriptures referred to in this book are taken from the most up to date translation of the New International Version of the Holy Bible published by Zondervan Publishing House and provided on-line by www.biblegateway.com

First published by Jacob's Well Publishing January 2017

ISBN-13:
978-0692818671 (Jacob's Well Publishing)

ISBN-10:
0692818677

Editing Consultant – Julie Keene
Cover Art provided by Gregg Olsen

12 Steps to "Truly Knowing" Jesus Christ

A down to earth commentary on:

How to work out your Salvation {with fear and trembling}

By: Pastor Charlie Haynes

Dedication

This book is first of all dedicated to my unbelievable and incredible family – specifically my wife Pam and my four children Virginia, Tammy, Susan and Asa – whose loving, forgiving and merciful hearts allowed me to retake a position as loving husband and father that I had foolishly thrown away and in no way deserved to be given back.

This book is further dedicated to the thousands of men and women and the families they represent that have been willing <u>FIRST</u> to share their hopelessness, their desperation, their fear and their failures with me but <u>SECOND</u> and most importantly to share their <u>VICTORIES</u> with me as they walked away from a life of drug addiction to take their rightful place in a new life in Christ.

This book is dedicated to those that have prayed prayers of protection over our ministry over the last sixteen years –knowing that we are rising to our feet <u>every</u> morning to fight the "good fight" against those things of Hell that are focused on destroying our families, our cities, our states and our nation.

But most of all this book is dedicated to my Lord and Savior Christ Jesus who loved me enough to suffer and die on the Cross of Calvary so that in spite of my sick and depraved behaviors in life, I could be forgiven. Without His direct intervention in my life NONE of the other dedications on this page would have been possible.

A little about the author: Pastor Charlie Haynes

I was born in Stamford, Texas in 1944 and shortly after moved to Meridian, Ms where I grew up. I attended Highland Elementary, Kate Griffin Jr. High, Meridian High School and went on to four years at Livingston State Teachers College in Livingston, Ala {now called UWA}.

After leaving college I entered the field of retail management with F.W. Woolworth, then Woolco, then TG& Y, then Walmart and finally Marvin's Home Center Stores. That career spanned over 30 years of my life. Early in my career {1966} I married my wife Pamela Smith Haynes from Shucktown, Ms. {that's right, she was a country girl}. We have four children - Virginia, Tammy, Susan and Asa.

Unfortunately for me and particularly for my wife and family I began a downward spiral over those 30 years that led me into behaviours centered totally around the lust of my eyes, the needs of my flesh and the pride of life that turned me into a dark and depraved man, husband and father.

In 1996 when my family could take it no longer, my wife asked me for a divorce and my children basically disowned me and then ordered me to get out and don't come back. Only then did I become willing to accept how deep into depravity I had sunk.

And just when I thought all was lost I met a man named Christ Jesus. He has not only saved me, saved my marriage and my family but He has literally transformed me into a totally new creation. What I once thought was the end of everything, I now know was the BEGINNING of everything.

Because I am so grateful for His mercy and loving kindness I have purposed along with my wife and family to spend the rest of my days on this earth sharing the Good News with hopeless and hurting individuals and families - that no matter how bad it seems - Christ can redeem it, heal it and restore it. Hence, my wife Pam and I founded Righteous Oaks Recovery Center for Men in Chunky, Ms in 2001 and Jacobs Well Recovery Center for Women in Poplarville, Ms in 2005 and most recently our second Men's Recovery Center called Damascus Road also in Poplarville, Ms.

Fun Things I Do: When I'm looking for something to pass the few leisure hours I have these days its going to generally be spending some quality time with my precious wife Pam or one of my kids or watching one of my 12 grand children or three great grandchildren as they grow. And, there is nothing like pushing out onto the little lake in front of my house and just spending some quality time with God.

Married to: Pamela {Smith} Haynes

Children: I have 4 children, 12 grandchildren and 3 great grandchildren.

Favorite Books (other than the Bible): Obviously, my favorite book is the Holy Bible. But I love surrounding myself with any and all other books that will lead me to a better understanding and daily application of His Word. I'm going to be surrounded by Bible Dictionaries, Concordances, Commentaries and writings of great men and women of God who know how to share, not only the theology of the Word, but the daily application of it.

Favorite TV Shows/Movies: I don't watch much television because honestly there is not much on that is worth looking at anymore but when I do, it will probably be the weather or the history channel.

My Heart's Desire: I live my life today with the assurance of my Salvation, the living proof of my transformation and a burning desire to rise from my bed every morning with only one prayer in my heart. "Lord, until you bring me home to be with you for eternity do not let one day go by that you do not place a broken hurting person in my path that I can give the same hope you have given me in Christ Jesus, Amen."

Foreword

<u>THE QUESTION OF THE DAY IS</u>:

"What do we have to do to prove we are a Christian and… "Who are we trying to prove it too?"

Most of us think that being a Christian means:

*Going to church on Sunday as often as we can {if not every Sunday at least on Easter and Christmas} and if we're "REALLY GOOD" Christians we will go EVERY Sunday and maybe even on a Sunday night or Wednesday night.

*We know were supposed to give some money to the church when they run that plate by us every Sunday cause after all they've got to pay the light bill and stuff and the preacher needs something for his trouble.

*We're pretty sure we need to worship in a Christ centered, Holy Ghost filled, Bible believing church where the pastor preaches fearlessly against sin and all the messages come directly from God's Word but, MORE IMPORTANTLY, we have to find a church that the shakers and movers attend, that has the fanciest facility, the most members, the most popular preacher, the biggest gym and fellowship hall and for sure the winningest church league soft ball and basketball team in town.

*We know that God expects us to spend some time in prayer ... especially WHEN THINGS AREN'T GOING WELL IN OUR LIVES or occasionally when we sit down to a meal with other folks WE THINK ARE CHRISTIANS.

*We know that we shouldn't cuss or tell off-color jokes or take the Lord's name in vain but we all know God's got a sense of humor right?

*We know that we should try to be nice to other people and we do try to AS LONG AS THEY'RE NICE TO US

*We know we shouldn't lie or cheat or steal or gossip or slander or run around on our spouse or disrespect our parents or any of that kind of stuff but "all have sinned and fallen short" right. People make mistakes - they just can't help it.

Maybe what you and I need to prove to all our friends and neighbors and co-workers that we REALLY ARE Christians is a "CHRISTIANITY KIT"

The Christianity Kit Would Contain These Items:

A Picture of Christ
A Fish Emblem
A Jesus Car Tag or Bumper Sticker
A Christian T-shirt
A Necklace with a Cross on it
A Huge Bible to put on our Coffee Table in the living room
A "As for me and my house" Door Mat
A Church Cook Book with one of our Recipes in it
A Certificate of Baptism
A Letter of Membership

A Perfect Attendance Pin
A Document Showing That We Are a Leader
in our Church

Oh yeah, all these things are great and they
may impress our friends, BUT, until we have
FIRST met "GOD'S DEFINITION OF
SALVATION" by receiving His Son Christ
Jesus as our personal Lord and Savior ...AND
THEN... are TRULY "BEARING THE FRUIT"
OF THAT RELATIONSHIP DAILY...

ALL THAT OTHER STUFF... DON'T MEAN
DIDLEY SQUAT!!!

You might want to read Christ's warning in:
Revelation 3:14-17

*14 ..."These are the words of the Amen, the faithful
and true witness, the ruler of God's creation. 15 I
know your deeds, that you are neither cold nor hot.
I wish you were either one or the other! 16 So,
because you are lukewarm — neither hot nor cold — I
am about to spit you out of my mouth. 17 YOU
SAY, 'I am rich; I have acquired wealth and do not
need a thing.' BUT you do not realize that you are
wretched, pitiful, poor, blind and naked.*

I was talking with a Pastor friend {who I respected very much} that pastored a very large denominational church in our community and I asked him about a Biblical subject that had troubled me for some time.

"Brother, do you believe in the doctrine of 'once saved always saved'?"

He smiled warmly – placed his hand on my shoulder and said, "No my friend – I believe in **'IF SAVED ALWAYS SAVED'."**

BINGO!!!

Anybody can run down to the altar in a church – at a tent revival – a summer camp ground meeting or some other religious gathering and state that Christ is Lord and millions have and then gone straight back to living their life like they are "going to hell in a hand basket." My friend that is NOT what true salvation looks like. That is simply an "intellectual agreement" with what the **world thinks** salvation and KNOWING JESUS CHRIST looks like.

I have come to believe through intensive Bible study and twenty years of constant observation of the disasters I have seen created in the lives of people who base their belief on who Christ Jesus really is and how eternal salvation works by what "MAN" says instead of what God's Word says that, coming to TRULY KNOW Jesus Christ and confirming your Salvation by way of His Blood sacrifice on Calvary is and always will be an ongoing daily process in your life here on earth.

That is why Philippians 2:12 (NIV) states boldly:
*12 Therefore, my dear friends, as you have always obeyed — not only in my presence, but now much more in my absence — **continue to work out your salvation with fear and trembling,***

The sobering fact is, that there is MUCH more to our successful daily relationship with Almighty God through Jesus Christ than most of us realize. BUT, if we take the time to search through the truth of God's Word, we will find all the requirements clarified in NUMEROUS scriptures.

Scriptures Like:

7 These people are springs without water and mists driven by a storm. Blackest darkness is reserved for them. 18 For they mouth empty, boastful words and, by appealing to the lustful desires of the flesh, they entice people who are just escaping from those who live in error. 19 They promise them freedom, while they themselves are slaves of depravity – for "people are slaves to whatever has mastered them." 20 If they have escaped the corruption of the world by knowing our Lord and Savior Jesus Christ and are again entangled in it and are overcome, they are worse off at the end than they were at the beginning. 21 It would have been better for them not to have known the way of righteousness, than to have known it and then to turn their backs on the sacred command that was passed on to them. 22 Of them the proverbs are true: "A dog returns to its vomit," and, "A sow that is washed returns to her wallowing in the mud."
2 Peter 2:17-22 (NIV)

Or this:

15 "Watch out for false prophets. They come to you in sheep's clothing, but inwardly they are ferocious wolves. 16 By their fruit you will recognize them. Do people pick grapes from thornbushes, or figs from thistles? 17 Likewise, every good tree bears good fruit, but a bad tree bears bad fruit. 18 A good tree cannot bear bad fruit, and a bad tree cannot bear good fruit. 19 Every tree that does not bear good fruit is cut down and thrown into the fire. 20 Thus, by their fruit you will recognize them. 21 "Not everyone who says to me, 'Lord, Lord,' will enter the kingdom of heaven, but only the one who does the will of my Father who is in heaven. 22 Many will say to me on that day, 'Lord, Lord, did we not prophesy in your name and in your name drive out demons and in your name perform many miracles?' 23 Then I will tell them plainly, 'I never knew you. Away from me, you evildoers!'
Matthew 7:15-23 (NIV)

And then this:

4 In the presence of God and of Christ Jesus, who will judge the living and the dead, and in view of his appearing and his kingdom, I give you this charge: 2 Preach the word; be prepared in season and out of season; correct, rebuke and encourage — with great patience and careful instruction. 3 For the time will come when people will not put up with sound doctrine. Instead, to suit their own desires, they will gather around them a great number of teachers to say what their itching ears want to hear. 4 They will turn their ears away from the truth and turn aside to myths. 5 But you, keep your head in all situations, endure hardship, do the work of an evangelist, discharge all the duties of your ministry.
2 Timothy 4:1-5 (NIV)

Or what about this dire warning about what will happen to "The Church"

23 Again the word of the LORD came to me: 24 "Son of man, say to the land, 'You are a land that has not been cleansed or rained on in the day of wrath.' 25 There is a conspiracy of her princes within her like a roaring lion tearing its prey; they devour people, take treasures and precious things and make many widows within her. 26 Her priests do violence to my law and profane my holy things; they do not distinguish between the holy and the common; they teach that there is no difference between the unclean and the clean; and they shut their eyes to the keeping of my Sabbaths, so that I am profaned among them. 27 Her officials within her are like wolves tearing their prey; they shed blood and kill people to make unjust gain. 28 Her prophets whitewash these deeds for them by false visions and lying divinations. They say, 'This is what the Sovereign LORD says' — when the LORD has not spoken. 29 The people of the land practice extortion and commit robbery; they oppress the poor and needy and mistreat the foreigner, denying them justice. 30 "I looked for someone among them who would build up the wall and stand before me in the gap on behalf of the land so I would not have to destroy it, but I found no one. 31 So I will pour out my wrath on them and consume them with my fiery anger, bringing down on their own heads all they have done, declares the Sovereign LORD."

Ezekiel 22:23-31 (NIV)

Table of Contents

STEP 1
HEARING ABOUT HIM

Most people when they are asked if they are "Christians" will say **YES** because, "logically speaking", they reason it out this way. Well, I was born and raised in the United States of America and the United States is considered a Christian nation therefore I can consider myself a Christian. I hate to be the bearer of sad tidings but where you were born {including the U.S.} has no bearing on whether or not you are, <u>in truth,</u> a Christian by God's definition.

Likewise, most people when asked if they "know" someone they will say **YES** but what they really mean is: "I have <u>heard</u> of them." There are millions and millions of people who profess that they know Jesus Christ and drop his name often if they think it can benefit them personally but the truth is they don't "really know him" at all.

The meaning of the phrase "TO KNOW" is: to have ALL the facts about something or someone and be certain those facts are true – to have the true information about – to have FIRMLY in mind – to have a full understanding, information or knowledge of – TO HAVE EXPERIENCE WITH – to be able to readily recognize and to be able to tell apart from others.

The <u>Biblical</u> meaning of the phrase "to know" is: to know <u>ABSOLUTELY</u>!!!

In the Book of John Chapter 1 verses 26 and 27 we hear John the Baptist say to the Church Leaders of his day:

*"I baptize with water but **among you stands one you do not know**. He is the one who comes after me' the thongs of whose sandals I am not worthy to untie."*

Even when Jesus was walking this earth physically, it would be fair to say that there were MANY more people who "heard of Him" than "actually knew Him." The Word tells us that today Christ Jesus does not physically walk among us as He did in the days of John the Baptist, but in these times He is seated at the right hand of the Father in the Kingdom of Heaven.

34 Who then is the one who condemns? No one. Christ Jesus who died — more than that, who was raised to life — is at the right hand of God and is also interceding for us.
Romans 8:34 NIV

The fact that He is no longer present on this earth so that we can physically meet Him or talk to Him or "hang out" with Him is no excuse for us to not "truly know Him."

Consider THESE Scriptures

18 The wrath of God is being revealed from heaven against all the godlessness and wickedness of people, who suppress the truth by their wickedness,

19 since what may be known about God is plain to them, because God has made it plain to them. 20 For since the creation of the world God's invisible qualities – his eternal power and divine nature – have been clearly seen, being understood from what has been made, <u>so that people are without excuse.</u>

21 For although they knew God, they neither glorified him as God nor gave thanks to him, but their thinking became futile and their foolish hearts were darkened. 22 Although they claimed to be wise, they became fools 23 and exchanged the glory of the immortal God for images made to look like a mortal human being and birds and animals and reptiles. 24 Therefore God gave them over in the sinful desires of their hearts to sexual impurity for the degrading of their bodies with one another. 25 They exchanged the truth about God for a lie, and worshiped and served created things rather than the Creator – who is forever praised. Amen. 26 Because of this, God gave them over to shameful lusts. Even their women exchanged natural sexual relations for unnatural ones. 27 In the same way the men also abandoned natural relations with women and were inflamed with lust for one another. Men committed shameful acts with other men, and received in themselves the due penalty for their error.

28 Furthermore, just as they did not think it worthwhile to retain the knowledge of God, so God gave them over to a depraved mind, so that they do what ought not to be done. 29 They have become filled with every kind of wickedness, evil, greed and depravity. They are full of envy, murder, strife, deceit and malice. They are gossips, 30 slanderers, God-haters, insolent, arrogant and boastful; they invent ways of doing evil; they disobey their parents; 31 they have no understanding, no fidelity, no love, no mercy. 32 Although they know God's righteous decree that those who do such things deserve death, they not only continue to do these very things but also approve of those who practice them.

Romans 1:18-32 (NIV)

When He left this earth to return to the Father He had firmly established His Word – His Will and His Way on earth so all men could walk in it.

How did He do that? Through the legacy of His time spent on this earth - through generational testimony of those who "truly knew Him" – through the legacy of His teaching left for us in the New Testament writings - and very importantly through the advice and counsel of the Holy Spirit of God that Christ has placed in us as our Heavenly Council and guide until he returns.

13 And you also were included in Christ when you heard the message of truth, the gospel of your salvation. When you believed, you were marked in him with a seal, the promised Holy Spirit, 14 who is a deposit guaranteeing our inheritance until the redemption of those who are God's possession – to the praise of his glory.
Ephesians 1:13-14 (NIV)

Having "TRULY BELIEVED" you will do this.....

16 So I say, walk by the Spirit, and you will not gratify the desires of the flesh. 17 For the flesh desires what is contrary to the Spirit, and the Spirit what is contrary to the flesh. They are in conflict with each other, so that you are not to do whatever

you want. [18] But if you are led by the Spirit {NOT MAN}, you are not under the law.
[19] The acts of the flesh are obvious: sexual immorality, impurity and debauchery; [20] idolatry and witchcraft; hatred, discord, jealousy, fits of rage, selfish ambition, dissensions, factions [21] and envy; drunkenness, orgies, and the like. I warn you, as I did before, that those who live like this will not inherit the kingdom of God. [22] But the fruit of the Spirit is love, joy, peace, forbearance, kindness, goodness, faithfulness, [23] gentleness and self-control. Against such things there is no law.
[24] Those who belong to Christ Jesus have crucified the flesh with its passions and desires. [25] Since we live by the Spirit, let us keep in step with the Spirit.
Galatians 5:16-25 (NIV)

God's Word tells us in Proverbs that He orders the steps of the Righteous. My experience in observing God's miraculous works over the last twenty years has shown me that He also "orders the steps" of those who are <u>BECOMING RIGHTEOUS</u>! Those who have "heard of Him" but have now begun to BELIEVE what they have heard are now ready to move to STEP 2.

STEP 2

My experience has been that when you begin to BELIEVE what you have HEARD, it produces the measure of FAITH to make you want to KNOW MORE and brings you to the next step on your journey to "TRULY KNOWING" Jesus Christ:

FINDING OUT ABOUT HIM....

[14] How, then, can they call on the one they have not believed in? And how can they believe in the one of whom they have not heard? And how can they hear without someone preaching to them? [15] And how can anyone preach unless they are sent? As it is written: "How beautiful are the feet of those who bring good news….. [17] Consequently, faith comes from hearing the message, and the message is heard through the Word about Christ.
Romans 10:14-17 (NIV)

You will find that gaining the tiniest measure of FAITH from beginning to BELIEVE what you have heard about Christ will birth a "MOUNTAINOUS DETERMINATION" and HUNGER FOR THE TRUTH" within you.

Consider these words

Now FAITH is being sure of what we hope for and certain of what we do not see.
Hebrews 11:1(NIV)

I remember early on in my walk toward an abiding and meaningful walk with Christ that the Holy Spirit cautioned me that that God could not use me if I continued to operate with HALF A FAITH.

When I said, "What do you mean Lord?"

He replied, "You are sure of what you hope for but you are not certain of what you can't see. You're still not sure I can deliver what I promise."

Then he shared these two awesome promises to me:

[20] *"Because you have so little faith. Truly I tell you, if you have faith as small as a mustard seed, you can say to this mountain, 'Move from here to there,' and it will move. Nothing will be impossible for you."*
Matthew 17:20 (NIV)

And then this...

[26] *Jesus looked at them and said, "With man this is impossible, but with God all things are possible."*
Matthew 19:26 (NIV)

So now filled with the FAITH and DETERMINATION to FIND OUT more about this 'man' Jesus Christ – What is the best way to go about it?

* "Spoon Feeding"- You must go quickly to a place where God's Word is regularly TAUGHT and PREACHED. But I don't mean just ANYWHERE His Word is taught and preached; I mean a PARTICULAR PLACE. I mean a place of Worship like the one the great Theologian E. W. Bullinger suggests:

"How to pick a Church"

"You ask, where you are to worship? We reply wherever God is glorified, Christ is exalted, God's Word is honored, the Holy Spirit's power is evidenced and man diminished. Never go anywhere where you do not know more of God's Word than when you entered. Never be IN any Body where you may be "turned out"; or have your name down where it may be scratched out.

Be content with the membership which God has given you in the Spiritual Unity of the Body of Christ, from which no power in Earth or Hell can cut you off and be content that your name was written in the Lamb's "book of life" before the foundation of the world, and from which no power in Earth or Hell can ever take it out. Do nothing to imply that you do not hold these priceless privileges to be of infinite value; or that they can be added to in the slightest degree by any of man's corporate unities."

-- Dr. E.W. Bullinger

Make sure the Pastor is a person you feel you can trust to speak in to your life in times of trouble – a person you can build a personal as well as a Spiritual relationship with. And make sure that the prayer that Pastor seeks from his congregation is exactly the same one the Apostle Paul sought from **his** congregation:

[19] *Pray also for me, that whenever I speak, words may be given me so that I will fearlessly make known the mystery of the gospel,* [20] *for which I am an ambassador in chains. Pray that I may declare it fearlessly, as I should.*
Ephesians 6:19-20 (NIV)

RUN OUT OF AND AWAY FROM AS QUICKLY AS POSSIBLE ANY CHURCH THAT HAS A POLITICALLY CORRECT PASTOR OR COOKIE CUTTER WORSHIP SERVICES

"Treasure Hunting" – Forming and maintaining an intensive routine of **daily** Bible reading and Bible study is critical to finding out who Jesus Christ is.

In the Book of Proverbs our Heavenly Father refers to Bible Study as a "Treasure Hunt":

> *2 My son, if you accept my words*
> *and store up my commands within you,*
> *2 turning your ear to wisdom*
> *and applying your heart to understanding –*
> *3 indeed, if you call out for insight*
> *and cry aloud for understanding,*
> *4 and if you look for it as for silver*
> *and search for it as for hidden treasure,*
> *5 then you will understand the fear of the LORD*
> *and find the knowledge of God.*
> **Proverbs 2:1-5 (NIV)**

We must come to understand and believe that Bible reading and Bible study are two distinctly different ways of "finding out about Christ" and the promise of Salvation He offers us.

Serious and comprehensive BIBLE STUDY daily will allow you to engrave the Word of God on your heart. An effective relationship with God through Christ is a "HEART THING" – not a "mind thing." You and I will NEVER be on an intellectual level with God. {although many theologians have tried}

8 *"For my thoughts are not your thoughts,*
neither are your ways my ways,"
declares the LORD.
9 *"As the heavens are higher than the earth,*
so are my ways higher than your ways
and my thoughts than your thoughts. 10 *As the*
rain and the snow
come down from heaven,
and do not return to it
without watering the earth
and making it bud and flourish,
so that it yields seed for the sower and bread for
the eater,
11 *so is my word that goes out from my mouth:*
It will not return to me empty,
but will accomplish what I desire
and achieve the purpose for which I sent it.
Isaiah 55:8-11 (NIV)

And then there is this awesome promise from God concerning having God's Word in your heart:

My son, do not forget my teaching,
but keep my commands in your heart,
2 for they will prolong your life many years
and bring you peace and prosperity. 3 Let love
and faithfulness never leave you;
bind them around your neck,
write them on the tablet of your heart.
4 Then you will win favor and a good name
in the sight of God and man.
Proverbs 3:1-4 (NIV)

Bible <u>STUDY</u> will require a little more time and effort on your part than simple Bible Reading. You may want to add to these requirements but at a minimum you should do this in preparation.

*Find a quiet space that you can retreat to for your time of Study.

*Do your best to make your study time uninterrupted and undistracted.

*The minimum study tools at your disposal should be a Life Application Bible **{the study notes at the beginning of each Book and Chapter in the Application type Bibles as well as the footnotes are invaluable to a serious student of the Word}**. Also, a Concordance, an Illustrated Bible Encyclopedia, and a Webster's Dictionary are very important. There may be other study helps you want to add but those are the most helpful in giving you a clearer understanding of what you are reading.

Contrary to what some religious folks might think, the goal of serious Bible Study is not to make you a walking talking Bible expert who can accurately quote a scripture on any subject at the drop of a hat. What you are doing is engraving the Truth of God so deeply and so indelibly in you that whatever choice comes before you in life {although you may not be able to remember what chapter and verse it came from} you will know **"in your heart"** without any doubt what Christ Jesus would want you to do in the circumstances.

Ok, so how is Bible **READING** different from Bible study and what are the benefits. Well, they are alike in that they are both Biblical "Treasure Hunts" but where in serious Bible **STUDY** we are searching for the Power and Truth of God's WORD – in Bible **READING** we are searching for the sound of **HIS VOICE** speaking directly into our Spirit. God's Word refers to this miraculous gift as "REVELATION KNOWLEDGE." Let me give you one Biblical example of this gift by sharing a scripture with you that not only talks about it but actually allowed me to experience it for myself.

13 When Jesus came to the region of Caesarea Philippi, he asked his disciples, "Who do people say the Son of Man is?"
14 They replied, "Some say John the Baptist; others say Elijah; and still others, Jeremiah or one of the prophets."
15 "But what about you?" he asked. "Who do you say I am?"
16 Simon Peter answered, "You are the Messiah, the Son of the living God." 17 Jesus replied, "Blessed are you, Simon son of Jonah, for this was not revealed to you by flesh and blood, but by my

Father in heaven. ¹⁸ *And I tell you that you are Peter, and on this rock I will build my church, and the gates of Hades will not overcome it.* ¹⁹ *I will give you the keys of the kingdom of heaven; whatever you bind on earth will be bound in heaven, and whatever you loose on earth will be loosed in heaven."*

Matthew 16:13-19 (NIV)

You can find all kinds of Theological commentaries and opinions on what verses 17 and 18 mean BUT I remember clearly how in a moment of Revelation God interpreted them to me as I read them. What He was saying to me was: "Charlie Haynes, I want you to understand that you will live a blessed and productive life if you grasp the critical importance of listening to what I SAY instead of what a FLESH AND BLOOD MAN SAYS. If you will place ALL your trust in the Truth of my Word as you STUDY it and respond with all your heart concerning to what I reveal to you while READING it, whatever you bind on earth will be bound in heaven, and whatever you loose on earth will be loosed in heaven."

I have done what He asked AND He has kept his Promise.

Let me share one more piece of advice about Bible reading. Each time just before you begin your daily Bible reading, bow your head – hold your bible against your heart and pray this simple prayer: "Father as I open this Bible tonight it is my fervent prayer that you will reveal something to my heart that will draw me closer to you in Christ Jesus and give me a greater understanding of your Word."

Do not close your Bible until He has answered your prayer.
{AND HERE IS WHY!}

12 For the Word of God is alive and active. Sharper than any double-edged sword, it penetrates even to dividing soul and spirit, joints and marrow; it judges the thoughts and attitudes of the heart.
Hebrews 4:12 (NIV)

Although millions of people around the world read the Bible every day {through the power of Revelation Knowledge} it speaks to each individual personally concerning what they are going through in that moment. No other writing in the history of the world can do that.

STEP 3
OK! YOU HEARD ABOUT HIM!
YOU FOUND OUT ABOUT HIM!
Now the next step:
SEEKING HIM!

Webster's definition of the word SEEK - to want to be in the presence of.

All of us have "heard about" someone in life but nothing ever came of it. Most of us have "heard about" someone that peaked our curiosity BUT on further examination it wasn't worth following up on. But ever-so often we hear about someone – then do a little follow up on what we have heard and – BINGO - we just want to go hang out with that someone and see if it's true. That's what happened to me when I heard about and went to the trouble to find out about Christ.

Let's start with a few important scriptures…

⁶ Seek the LORD while he may be found;
call on him while he is near.
⁷ Let the wicked forsake their ways
and the unrighteous their thoughts.
Let them turn to the LORD, and he will have mercy
on them,
and to our God, for he will freely pardon.
Isaiah 55:6-7 (NIV)

I am sure you must have heard the old religious cliché:

"PRAISE THE LORD-I FOUND JESUS"

NO – actually Jesus found ME. Jesus was never lost. Jesus always wanted to be with me. He was always SEEKING me. Jesus does not like to play hide and seek because He sees everything. It was ME who was hiding in a closet in the Pit of Hell playing hide and seek with Him.

¹⁶ You did not choose me, but I chose you and appointed you so that you might go and bear fruit – fruit that will last – and so that whatever you ask in my name the Father will give you.
John 15:16 (NIV)

It's always been Christ waiting on us-NOT us waiting on Him.

⁹ "So I say to you: Ask and it will be given to you; seek and you will find; knock and the door will be opened to you. ¹⁰ For everyone who asks receives; the one who seeks finds; and to the one who knocks, the door will be opened.
Luke 11:9-10 (NIV)

In my old life {before I met Christ} I spent a lot of my time "seeking stuff." Most of the time it was something that appealed to the "needs of my flesh – the lust of my eyes or the pride of life."

I was only interested in energetically **SEEKING** those things that I knew would benefit me personally but - {I'm sure none of you ever lived like that.}

The one thing I was always **SEEKING** was a better job than the one I had or a promotion on the one I was working. Of course my main concern when **SEEKING** a new job or taking a promotion was {that's right} "WHAT WERE THE BENEFITS"!!!

So, what ARE the benefits of SEEKING the truths that will lead you to "truly knowing" Christ? Just for starters I can tell you that you would find yourself living a life above and beyond anything you could have ever dreamed of. Check out THIS scripture:

9 However, as it is written:
"No eye has seen,
no ear has heard,
and no human mind has conceived" -
the things God has prepared for those who love
him —
1 Corinthians 2:9 (NIV)

Let's talk a little more specifically about just a few of the BENEFITS mentioned in God's Word that come directly from SEEKING Christ.

*3 Praise be to the God and Father of our Lord Jesus Christ, **who has blessed us <u>in the heavenly realms</u> with every spiritual blessing in Christ.***

Hallelujah! Right out of the box God's Word promises that through our relationship with Christ we are going to be BLESSED with what – with <u>every</u> spiritual blessing – AND that's a <u>lot</u> of blessing. But notice that the Word says we will be blessed in the "heavenly realms", NOT the "earthly realms."

In other words, in order for us to receive God's abundant blessings, we must consider ourselves Kingdom citizens NOT earthly citizens. We must have the mindset that we are not citizens of this world but we are just placed here by our Heavenly father to accomplish His will for our life before we return home to be with Him for eternity.

That's why when the disciples asked Jesus to teach them HOW to pray – He replied to them in Matthew 6 Verse 10 that one of the things they should pray is:

*"Your Kingdom come, your will be done,
on earth as it is in Heaven."*

You don't have to be in Heaven to be a Heavenly citizen.

4 For <u>he chose us</u> in him before the creation of the world to be holy and blameless in his sight.

You and I are not just some "Joe Blow from Kokomo." We were hand-picked by our Creator before we were knit in our mother's womb to be born into this world and live a righteous life; <u>AND</u> as long as we have breath in our body we can turn from our sinful life and become that holy and blameless man or woman in Christ.

In love 5 <u>he predestined us</u> for adoption to sonship through Jesus Christ, in accordance with his pleasure and will — 6 to the praise of his glorious grace, which he has freely given us in the One he loves.

You and I were born with a DESTINY – a destiny to become sons and daughters of the living God. He has sent us to this earth to step into that destiny so that He might be glorified.

Well Brother Charlie, how do I find out what **MY DESTINY** is?

The answer: READ –STUDY and APPLY Romans 12:1-2 immediately and consistently to your life here on earth.

Therefore, I urge you, brothers and sisters, in view of God's mercy, to offer your bodies as a living sacrifice, holy and pleasing to God – this is your true and proper worship. [2] Do not conform to the pattern of this world, but be transformed by the renewing of your mind. Then you will be able to test and approve what God's will is – his good, pleasing and perfect will.

[7] In him <u>we have redemption</u> through his blood,

Have you ever had to go to a Pawn Shop to "hock" something really valuable to get yourself out of a "pinch"? I have – and most of the time I wound up losing it because I couldn't afford the payments to get it back.

I remember an incident that happened once at our first men's recovery center called Righteous Oaks. One of the men who had come into the program came to me one morning and told me that by trade he was a certified automobile mechanic – and a good one. He went on to say that because of his heavy drug use he had "hocked" all his mechanic's tools in the pawn shop to get more drugs. He said, I don't have any way to get them back BUT if you would go down and **redeem them** and get them back for me, I could fix all the ministry's cars and trucks while I am here in the program and it won't cost you anything.

So, knowing what his giftings and equippings were and wanting to help him return to his destiny, **I went and "paid the price" for him.** All he had to do then was go to the pawn shop and take his tools back. How stupid would it have been then if he had said: "Thank you for paying the price Brother Charlie but I think I will just leave the tools at the pawn shop and let somebody else have them?

That incident carried me back to the memory of a significant moment in my "old life." One day as I sat somewhere pondering how bad things were going for me and what I was going to be able to do about it, God spoke something into my spirit that rocked my world.

He said: "Charlie Haynes, you have taken the priceless gifts of Destiny and Eternal Salvation that I gave you at birth and 'hocked' them in the Pawn Shop of life for pennies on the dollar."

And I said: "Lord what can I do? I don't have any way to get them back." And almighty God, knowing MY giftings and equippings and wanting to ME to have my Destiny back said, "I will redeem them for you but YOU will have to decide if you are willing to take them back."

AND HE REDEEMED THEM!

16 For God so loved the world that He gave his one and only Son, that whoever believes in him shall not perish but have eternal life. 17 For God did not send his Son into the world to condemn the world, but to save the world through him. 18 Whoever believes in him is not condemned, but whoever does not believe stands condemned already because they have not believed in the name of God's one and only Son.
John 3:16-18 (NIV)

{He has given us} the forgiveness of sins, in accordance with the riches of God's grace 8 that he lavished on us. With all wisdom and understanding,

There is no greater gift that has ever been given by our Father in Heaven than the gift of forgiveness that comes from the sacrifice of Christ Jesus on the Cross of Calvary. You and I will never receive any gift from any other person greater than the gift of forgiveness. And you will never be able to give anyone else a greater gift than the gift of forgiveness. I believe that UN-FORGIVENESS is the most dangerous "disease" on earth. Yes I said "DISEASE."

Some time when you have a few minutes just sit down at your computer and "google" – **the health risks of un-forgiveness** and see what comes up. You might think you are going to see a bunch of sermons on the subject by well-known Preachers, BUT, what you are actually going to see is dozens of papers written by well-known psychologist and psychiatrists warning of its dangers. Here is just one little sample:

The Power of Forgiveness {by Judith Perlman}

As a psychotherapist specializing in health psychology for over twenty years, I've come to understand that in order to live fully and joyfully in the present, it is absolutely necessary to release the pain that we all carry with us from the past.

Without the power of forgiveness to help us heal, the past has the potential to destroy our present lives. Giving up the pain of the past is not easy -- but it is one of the keys to a healthy life.

THE HEALTH BENEFITS OF FORGIVENESS

Research has shown that no matter how awful the offense, the ability to forgive is a technique that can be learned. And learning to forgive can...

- lower your blood pressure,
- improve immune system response,
- reduce anxiety and depression,
- improve your sleep,
- improve self-esteem and sense of empowerment,
- help you to have more rewarding relationships, both professionally and personally,
- reduce stress by releasing toxic emotions,
- reduce dysfunctional patterns of behavior,
- increase energy for living and healing,
- improve relationships and social integration,
- increase peace of mind,
- aid peaceful death.

Holding un-forgiveness against someone else is like you drinking the poison hoping the other person will die.

Chronic anger, hurt, guilt, hostility can have a debilitating effect on us. These toxic emotions create an avalanche of stress hormones. For instance, cortisol makes you feel speeded up, tense and overwhelmed. Over the long run, heightened cortisol levels impact the immune system. And recent brain research has demonstrated that excess cortisol levels impair your cognitive ability and damage cells in the memory centers of your brain.

I think it's it is important for you to know that there are four different kinds of forgiveness and YOU control three of them.

The first is the forgiveness of God. When you fall on your knees in a moment of Godly sorrow – **confess** the sin of your life before Him – **repent** of those sins and receive Christ as your personal Lord and Savior - God will forgive the sin of your past right there and then.

The second is forgiving yourself for the sin of your past. Failing to forgive yourself after God has forgiven you is an abomination to Him. It is like you saying: "You know what Lord, that Blood your Son shed on the Cross of Calvary, that wasn't good enough to cover **MY** sin.

Then third is you being willing to fully forgive those who have hurt you. Here you go...

> [14] *For if you forgive other people when they sin against you, your heavenly Father will also forgive you.* [15] *But if you do not forgive others their sins, your Father will not forgive your sins.*
> **Matthew 6:14-15 (NIV)**

The only forgiveness you DO NOT control is having someone else forgive you for the wrongs you have done to them. Don't worry about those either. Just lay them at the Foot of the Cross and if God thinks it is important that it happen – He will make it happen.

²⁸ And we know that in all things God works for the good of those who love him, who have been called according to his purpose.
Romans 8:28 (NIV)

⁹ he made known to us the mystery of his will according to his good pleasure, which he purposed in Christ, ¹⁰ to be put into effect when the times reach their fulfillment – to bring unity to all things in heaven and on earth under Christ.

The Holy Bible is not some mysterious document dropped off here by aliens thousands of years ago that only highly trained theological minds can comprehend. The Bible is the greatest self-help book ever written. It was written **FOR** you. It was written **ABOUT** you. And it was written **BECAUSE** of you. Even better than all that it was written by The One who created you. The One who has been observing the slip falls and failures of those He created since time began. If you will simply take the time to begin to seriously read and study it, you will find that He will caution you in advance concerning every bad choice you can make in life. And if you make that mistake anyway, He will show you the way out of it. You don't even have to read it all the way through before you can start the journey to your new life in Christ. Just start in Genesis Chapter 1 and start reading. When you run across something you are doing that God says **you shouldn't be doing** – QUIT DOING IT!!! And if you run across something God says **you should be doing** but you are not – GET TO DOING IT!!!

[11] In him we were also <u>chosen</u> having been predestined according to the plan of him who works out everything in conformity with the purpose of his will, [12] in order that we, who were the first to put our hope in Christ, might be for the praise of his glory.

If you were to get your concordance and see what the Greek word in the original writings in Ephesians 1:4 was you would see that the Greek word used for "<u>chose us</u>" meant "PICKED." But the Greek word for the phrase "<u>also chosen</u>" in the verse used in Ephesians 1:11 meant "SENT." Let me illustrate the point concerning the difference in these two verses this way:

When I was a kid growing up, one of our favorite things to do each weekend was to get a bunch of boys together from the neighborhood and go play some sand lot baseball. How that was generally done was that we would all meet in an empty lot and the two oldest boys in the group would assume the position of team captains. There would be the ceremonial "bat toss and grab" to see which one would get the first pick of the boys available and then the "PICKING" would begin.

To be picked first by one of the team captains was a HUGE honor because that meant you were one heck of a ball player. Let's say I was one of the boys picked first {<u>NOT</u>} and now we are pulled to the side by the team captain to be given our place on the team and the team captain **<u>sends</u>** me to play right field –

But I say to the captain, "I don't want to be right fielder I want to be pitcher."

Then the captain smiles warmly and says: "I'm the one doing the picking and the sending today and if you want to play on my team you will have to play where I send you. And then I poke my lip out and grab my bat and my ball and go home."

THAT my friend is how the kingdom of God works. HE picks your Destiny and HE sends you to your Destiny and if you don't want to go, you can take your Spiritual ball and bat and go home {and many of us have}. God has got plenty of folks on the sidelines that will be happy to step up and take your place.

13 And you also were included in Christ when you heard the message of truth, the gospel of your salvation. When you believed, you were marked in him with a seal, the promised Holy Spirit, 14 who is a deposit guaranteeing our inheritance until the redemption of those who are God's possession – to the praise of his glory.
Ephesians 1:3-14 (NIV)

There is no doubt in my mind, heart, soul or spirit that the greatest benefit we have received through "Truly Knowing" Christ is the forgiveness of our sins given to us by our Heavenly Father because His Son was willing to die for our sin and our sake on Calvary.

In my life I place the second greatest benefit in having received the Holy Spirit of God. If you want, to you can wade off into all kinds of arguments made by "Denominational Thinkers" and "Theological Geniuses" about what has to manifest itself in you or around you before you can "prove" you have the Holy Spirit in you. Don't get caught up in that!

Hold on a minute. Now I've got to stop and chase a rabbit.

I HATE DENOMINATIONALISM!!!

IT SEPERATES US AS TRUE CHRISTIANS AND MAKES US INEFFECTIVE AS SOLDIERS IN THE ARMY OF GOD.

Listen to what Christ said to the Samaritan Woman at the Well.

19 "Sir," the woman said, "I can see that you are a prophet. 20 Our ancestors worshiped on this mountain, but you Jews claim that the place where we must worship is in Jerusalem."
21 "Woman," Jesus replied, "believe me, a time is coming when you will worship the Father neither on this mountain nor in Jerusalem. 22 You Samaritans worship what you do not know; we worship what we do know, for salvation is from the Jews. 23 Yet a time is coming and has now come when the "true worshipers" will worship the Father in the Spirit and in truth, for they are the kind of worshipers the Father seeks. 24 God is spirit, and his worshipers must worship in the Spirit and in truth."
John 4:19-24 (NIV)

OK, I'm sorry I had to take that hard left there – just had to get that off my chest. NOW- let's get back to the subject at hand and THAT is talking about the benefit of receiving the Holy Spirit.

Ephesians 1:13-14 {above} tells me that when I received Christ as my personal Lord and Savior He placed in me {as God's possession} a "deposit" guaranteeing my inheritance in the Kingdom of Heaven until the time of redemption has come. That "deposit" was and is the Holy Spirit of God.

This is what Christ promised me in His Word that the benefits of that "deposit" would be for me while I am on this earth.

{This is what Jesus said to His Disciples concerning the coming of Holy Spirit} now I am going to him who sent me. None of you asks me, 'Where are you going?' 6 Rather, you are filled with grief because I have said these things. 7 But very truly I tell you, it is for your good that I am going away. Unless I go away, the Advocate will not come to you; but if I go, I will send him to you. 8 When he comes, he will prove the world to be in the wrong about sin and righteousness and judgment: 9 about sin, because people do not believe in me; 10 about righteousness, because I am going to the Father, where you can see me no longer; 11 and about judgment, because the prince of this world {Satan} now stands condemned.

12 "I have much more to say to you, more than you can now bear. 13 But when he, the Spirit of truth, comes, he will guide you into all the truth. He will not speak on his own; he will speak only what he hears, and he will tell you what is yet to come. 14 He will glorify me because it is from me that he will receive what he will make known to you. 15 All that belongs to the Father is mine. That is why I said the Spirit will receive from me what he will make known to you."

John 16:5-15 (NIV)

And then there is this:

*15 "If you love me, keep my commands. 16 And I will ask the Father, and he will give you another advocate to help you and be with you forever —
17 the Spirit of truth. The world cannot accept him, because it neither sees him nor knows him. But you know him, for he lives with you and will be in you.*

John 14:15-17 (NIV)

And finally this:

22 But the fruit {benefit} of the Spirit is love, joy, peace, forbearance, kindness, goodness, faithfulness, 23 gentleness and self-control. Against such things there is no law. 24 Those who belong to Christ Jesus have crucified the flesh with its passions and desires. 25 Since we live by the Spirit, let us keep in step with the Spirit. 26 Let us not become conceited, provoking and envying each other.
Galatians 5:22-26 (NIV)

WELL, we have sought Christ in this Chapter and although we could point to MANY more benefits that come from "Truly Knowing" him we have already found out that by being in a relationship with Him we are: BLESSED, CHOSEN, PREDESTINED, SENT, ADOPTED, REDEEMED, FORGIVEN, ENLIGHTENED, INCLUDED, AND FILLED WITH THE HOLY SPIRIT OF GOD.

And as if that wasn't enough...

The Holy Spirit brings with His indwelling: LOVE, JOY, PEACE, FORBEARANCE, KINDNESS, GOODNESS, FAITHFULLNESS, GENTLENESS, and SELF-CONTROL.

Folks, at this point I had heard enough to go to Step 4 – I hope you are ready to go with me.

STEP 4
OK! YOU HEARD ABOUT HIM!
YOU FOUND OUT ABOUT HIM!
YOU HAVE BEEN SEEKING HIM!
Now the next step:
MEETING HIM!

Whenever I am engaged in Spiritual Counseling with someone concerning the struggles they are going through, at some point, I am going to ask them straight up if they are "saved." If they <u>hesitate</u> or give me the slightest indication that they are not sure how to answer the question – I know immediately we have a problem. A man or woman who has TRULY accepted Jesus Christ as their personal Lord and Savior {gotten saved} have **no doubt** about it. The experience is carved in to their heart, mind, soul and spirit and they recognize the moment that it happened as **<u>THE</u>** turning point in their life.

I wrote this book because, sadly, I have met hundreds of men and women "who know that they know" they have accepted Christ as their Savior but they can't understand why it hasn't made a measurable difference in their lives.

I am trying to help people understand that Christ is not just the conductor on the "Let's all go to Heaven Train" and once He punches your ticket – you're home free.

There is no more moving account ever given of MEETING CHRIST – TURNING FROM YOUR SIN – AND ASSURING YOUR SALVATION – than what happened to Saul of Tarsus on the Damascus Road chronicled in Acts 9:10-20.

Look at this with me for a moment.

Saul's Conversion

As we begin to look at these scriptures I think it is important to make the point to those that may not be familiar with this story that Saul of Tarsus fully believed in God but he had made up his mind that this Jesus guy going around calling himself the Son of God and Savior of the world was a 'nut case" and deserved to be crucified because He was guilty of "blaspheming.

So Saul has decided at this point to spend the rest of his life rounding up anyone who called themselves a follower of Jesus Christ and turning them over to the religious authorities to be "eliminated."

9 Meanwhile, Saul was still breathing out murderous threats against the Lord's disciples. He went to the high priest ² and asked him for letters to the synagogues in Damascus, so that if he found any there who belonged to the Way {Christians}, whether men or women, he might take them as prisoners to Jerusalem. ³ As he neared Damascus on his journey, suddenly a light from heaven flashed around him. ⁴ He fell to the ground and heard a voice say to him, "Saul, Saul, why do you persecute me?"

THIS is what truly <u>MEETING CHRIST</u> for the first time looks like – feels like - and sounds like. Blinded by the "Light of the TRUTH of who you are – what you have allowed yourself to become and what you have done with your life will literally "KNOCK YOU OFF YOUR HIGH HORSE" and I guarantee you that you will NEVER forget that moment.

⁵ "Who are you, Lord?" Saul asked. "I am Jesus, whom you are persecuting," he replied.

Saul is right in the middle of a major REVELATION. It has just inescapably dawned on Him that he was obviously dead wrong about who Jesus Christ and those who followed Him were. You see Saul was one of those "Yea, I've HEARD OF HIM" guys that never thought it was worthwhile to find out about Him or seek Him. And now Saul has become the unsuspecting recipient of a true "COME TO JESUS" meeting

6 *"Now get up and go into the city, and you will be told what you must do."*

Verse 6 {above} is a powerful and important verse.

You see, when we <u>truly</u> first meet Christ, one of the first things that must happen is that we must be immediately ready to follow his commands. Christ says in John 14:15, "If you love me, you will obey what I command."

Saul could have simply done what so many of us have done when we met Jesus. He could have simply stood to his feet – dusted himself off – jumped on his horse – said "forget you Jesus" and took off down the road to go round up and kill some more Christians. Thank God that is NOT what he did and I pray to God that is not what you will do.

7 The men traveling with Saul stood there speechless; they heard the sound but did not see anyone.

I have never seen God, but I have heard the "Sound of His Voice" many times through the Power of the Holy Spirit since I met Jesus Christ.

8 Saul got up from the ground, but when he opened his eyes he could see nothing. So they led him by the hand into Damascus. 9 For three days he was blind, and did not eat or drink anything.

Saul had lived most of his life "blinded." He was blinded by his religiosity. He was blinded by his personal prejudices. He was blinded by his high opinion of himself. He was blinded by his position of power over others. He was blinded by his lack of knowledge concerning the Power of Christ. For this moment it became critical that he become blinded to everything **he thought he knew** to be able to see those things **he had never known.** Romans 11:32 tells us that: "God has turned all men over to disobedience so that He may have mercy on them." And even in Saul's temporary dilemma – MERCY was already on the way.

10 In Damascus there was a disciple named Ananias. The Lord called to him in a vision, "Ananias!"
"Yes, Lord," he answered.
11 The Lord told him, "Go to the house of Judas on Straight Street and ask for a man from Tarsus named Saul, for he is praying. 12 In a vision he has seen a man named Ananias come and place his hands on him to restore his sight."

The minute we come to the place where we are willing to say NO to the things of the world and YES to God – GOD MOVES. Because Saul was finally brought face to face with the truth about Christ, he found himself on his knees crying out to that same Savior he had so mistakenly denied. And in the midst of that repentant prayer, Christ placed a promise in his heart that help and healing were on the way.

He made that very same promise to me in a moment of brokenness over twenty years ago when the "Ananias" he sent to me to give me that same comfort was my twenty-two year old son Asa.

13 "Lord," Ananias answered, "I have heard many reports about this man and all the harm he has done to your holy people in Jerusalem. 14 And he has come here with authority from the chief priests to arrest all who call on your name."
*15 But the Lord said to Ananias, "Go! **This man is my chosen instrument** to proclaim my name to the Gentiles and their kings and to the people of Israel. 16 I will show him how much he must suffer for my name."*

Say WHAT??? God is going to take a man who has openly demeaned, cursed and blasphemed his "only begotten Son" and gleefully rounded up his followers to have them tortured and killed and make him "His chosen instrument" to go out into the world and preach the Gospel of Jesus Christ??? Wait a minute – that question sounds familiar.

Oh, no wonder – that's the same question I asked about MYSELF when this sick, perverted, depraved, alcoholic, pill head, lying, manipulating fool heard God say: "Charlie Haynes, I am about to make you my chosen instrument to carry the Good News to other "jacked up people" that no matter how bad the circumstances look, If you will trust me, I can and will fix it. And now twenty years in the ministry and having founded and operated three very successful Addiction Recovery Centers, you can bet I am a **BELIEVER.**

NO ONE is disqualified because of their past sins {no matter how egregious} from becoming the "chosen instrument" of God.

Just go back and study the old behaviors of EVERY Old Testament character that God delivered from their sinful lives and then used for miraculous works. As a matter of fact one of God's favorite things to do is to take "jacked up" people and make them "chosen instruments" of his will. Want proof? Then read this scripture:

26 Brothers and sisters, think of what you were when you were called. Not many of you were wise by human standards; not many were influential; not many were of noble birth. 27 But God chose the foolish things of the world to shame the wise; God chose the weak things of the world to shame the strong. 28 God chose the lowly things of this world and the despised things – and the things that are not – to nullify the things that are, 29 so that no one may boast before him.
1 Corinthians 1:26-29 (NIV)

I've been a "foolish thing" – Have you?

[17] Then Ananias went to the house and entered it. Placing his hands on Saul, he said, "Brother Saul, the Lord — Jesus, who appeared to you on the road as you were coming here — has sent me so that you may see again and be filled with the Holy Spirit." [18] Immediately, something like scales fell from Saul's eyes, and he could see again. He got up and was baptized, [19] and after taking some food, he regained his strength.

HALLELUJAH! PROMISE MADE – PROMISE KEPT!

Saul spent several days with the disciples in Damascus. [20] At once he began to preach in the synagogues that Jesus is the Son of God.
Acts 9:1-20 (NIV)

Many Bible Commentaries agree that Saul of Tarsus was recognized by his peers as one of the most highly educated and knowledgeable Bible Scholars of his time PRIOR TO meeting Christ on the Damascus Road.

Generally the only person who was considered superior to him Biblically was <u>his</u> mentor and teacher Gamaliel. However, this most brilliant mind said <u>this</u> about what he once thought he knew about religious matters:

2 And so it was with me, brothers and sisters. When I came to you, I did not come with eloquence or human wisdom as I proclaimed to you the testimony about God. 2 For I resolved to know nothing while I was with you except Jesus Christ and him crucified. 3 I came to you in weakness with great fear and trembling. 4 My message and my preaching were not with wise and persuasive words, but with a demonstration of the Spirit's power, 5 so that your faith might not rest on human wisdom, but on God's power.
1 Corinthians 2:1-5 (NIV)

Saul of Tarsus, the <u>misguided zealot,</u> upon meeting Christ on the Damascus Road became the Apostle Paul the <u>chosen instrument</u> and not only spent the rest of his time on this earth laying down his life for Jesus Christ also became the writer of most of the New Testament Books that you and I read and study today.

Christ doesn't pull any punches in God's Word about what it is going to be like if you determine to follow him.

Consider this…

> [34] *Then he called the crowd to him along with his disciples and said: "Whoever wants to be my disciple must deny themselves and take up their cross and follow me.* [35] *For whoever wants to save their life will lose it, but whoever loses their life for me and for the gospel will save it.* [36] *What good is it for someone to gain the whole world, yet forfeit their soul?* [37] *Or what can anyone give in exchange for their soul?* [38] *If anyone is ashamed of me and my words in this adulterous and sinful generation, the Son of Man will be ashamed of them when he comes in his Father's glory with the holy angels."*
> **Mark 8:34-38 (NIV)**

And this…

11 "Blessed are you when people insult you, persecute you and falsely say all kinds of evil against you because of me. 12 Rejoice and be glad, because great is your reward in heaven, for in the same way they persecuted the prophets who were before you.
Matthew 5:11-12 (NIV)

And this...

18 When Jesus saw the crowd around him, he gave orders to cross to the other side of the lake. 19 Then a teacher of the law came to him and said, "Teacher, I will follow you wherever you go."
20 Jesus replied, "Foxes have dens and birds have nests, but the Son of Man has no place to lay his head."
Matthew 8:18-20 (NIV)

STEP 5

OK! YOU HEARD ABOUT HIM!
YOU FOUND OUT ABOUT HIM!
YOU HAVE BEEN SEEKING HIM!
YOU HAVE MET HIM!

Now the next step:
ACCEPTING HIM!

You can go through the first four steps toward "TRULY KNOWING" Christ but STILL decide not to ACCEPT Him as your PERSONAL Lord and Savior and unfortunately many people have made that mistake.

Even having an encounter upon meeting Him as Saul did in the previous chapter does not seal the divine relationship you must have with Christ to carry you forward in the process of truly "walking out" your Salvation.

There is a "Covenant Agreement" that must be established between you and Christ before He will begin to pour out His Abundant Blessings of Joy and Peace and Healing and Reconciliation and Prosperity on you.

The terms of that Covenant are clearly outlined in God's Word in the Book of Romans when it says:

8 But what does it {the Word} say? "The word is near you; it is in your mouth and in your heart," that is, the message concerning the faith that we proclaim: 9 If you declare with your mouth, "Jesus is Lord," and believe in your heart that God raised him from the dead, you will be saved.
10 For it is with your heart that you believe and are justified, and it is with your mouth that you profess your faith and are saved. 11 As Scripture says, "Anyone who believes in him will never be put to shame." 12 For there is no difference between Jew and Gentile — the same Lord is Lord of all and richly blesses all who call on him, 13 for, "Everyone who calls on the name of the Lord will be saved."
Romans 10:8-13 (NIV)

VERY IMPORTANT! Walking carefully and thoughtfully through the first four steps of coming to "Truly Know" Christ have brought you to a place of FAITH, BELIEF and ASSURANCE of who Jesus REALLY is and who YOU really want to become so that you are NOW ready to ACCEPT HIM. And that means that you are ready to accept Him and live for Him from this day forward on HIS TERMS.

So let's talk a minute about the seriousness and meaning of the Covenant agreement you are about to make. This is an intimate, personal, one on one promise being made by you and you alone to your Creator concerning your relationship with His Son who has died on the Cross of Calvary for YOUR sins. Billy Graham can't save you. T D Jakes can't save you. Jessie Duplantis can't save you. I can't save you. This is between you and Jesus. So let's see what you are promising. You are about to "confess with your mouth" that you are agreeing to make Christ "LORD" of your life. That may sound easy to "declare" but you better make sure you understand what a "LORD" is.

**Webster's Definition of the word LORD
- One who has complete authority,
control, or power over others; a master
or ruler.**

You are making a covenant promise to your Heavenly Father that you are giving Christ through the Word of God and the leading of His Holy Spirit in you - total and complete authority, control and power over your life. In other words you are saying everything, every daily choice about how you live your life, where you go and who you fellowship with will now be determined by what Christ thinks NOT what you think. That is a BIG promise BUT if you aren't going to keep it, don't make it.

You are further saying that you "believe in your heart" that God raised Christ from the dead. It takes sincere FAITH to believe that miracle and just saying the words won't cut it. WHY? Because of the power of this verse which says:

*[10] For it is **<u>with your heart</u>** that you believe and are justified, and it is with your mouth that you profess your faith and are saved.*

It is important to understand that while you are making this covenant agreement, God is examining your heart {true intentions} so if you're not deadly serious about the promise – to God – it <u>AINT</u> Salvation.

STEP 6

OK! YOU HEARD ABOUT HIM!
YOU FOUND OUT ABOUT HIM!
YOU HAVE BEEN SEEKING HIM!
YOU HAVE MET HIM!
YOU HAVE ACCEPTED HIM!
Now the next step:
GETTING TO KNOW HIM!

Life has taught me that the only way I can "Truly Know" something is to EXPERIENCE IT. If I'm going to have someone work on my car, my household wiring or plumbing or maybe **operate** on me at a hospital – I don't want somebody that all they have done in life is read or study about it. I want somebody that also has EXPERIENCE doing it.

I feel the same way about my relationships with other people. I don't jump into important personal relationship with others until I get to know them myself through spending time with them.

¹⁴ But as for you, continue in what you have learned and have become convinced of, because you know those from whom you learned it
2 Timothy 3:14 (NIV)

**Webster's definition of the word:
KNOW - to perceive or understand as fact or truth; to apprehend clearly and with certainty.**

I can say with unwavering certainty that I personally "KNOW" Jesus Christ because I have <u>experienced</u> Him. I have experienced the fulfillment of every promise He has made me. And I have born witness to His miraculous healing and redemptive works for twenty years - not only in my own life and family but in our Addiction Recovery Center Graduates as well.

How do we REALLY get to know someone once we have met and accepted them into our life? Simple. We spend as much time as we can with them learning more and more about them.

The same principle applies to getting to know Christ; except, unlike most people we meet, He is not physically present in our life but rather He is Spiritually present. So let me spend a few minutes suggesting to you how to experience him and TRULY come to know Him Spiritually.

First: Be in your Bible every day reading and studying about Him specifically. For you to get to know Him best, let me strongly suggest that you make the New Testament Books of the Gospels {that would be Matthew, Mark, Luke and John} a specific goal of your regular reading and study plan. These are the accounts of the life of Jesus from before He was born until his death and resurrection at Calvary as well as the eye witness accounts of his Ministry and his miraculous works done while He was still on this Earth.

And I further strongly suggest that you concentrate more heavily in those places where Christ Himself is speaking.

Most modern Bibles have the Words of Christ printed boldly in red as a clear signal to you that this is Christ talking DIRECTLY to you. Pay very careful attention to everything He says and do everything in your power to keep your covenant promise to live by it.

Second: Counselors will be the first to tell you that the quickest way you can tell when a relationship is breaking down is when people stop talking to each other. If you don't have a burning desire to talk to Christ <u>every</u> day then you don't really want to have a relationship with or get to know Him any better.

PRAYER is the way we have Spiritual fellowship with Christ. You can talk to Him ANYTIME – riding in your car, sitting in a boat fishing, relaxing on your front porch, pushed back in your recliner or laying in your bed – He is always ready to converse with you. Don't make it hard. All it is - is talking to the best friend you have ever had.

Third: Be aware and recognize when He is actively working in the circumstances of your life or your family or your acquaintances. If you do, you are going to see healing and restoration and impossible things accomplished in your life and the lives of those around you as you walk out this relationship.

Things will happen that seem so impossible that you will just shake your head and say to yourself: "That had to be God."

Fourth: If you wanted to become a Bass Pro, would you seek advice from a kid sitting on a creek bank fishing with a safety pin hook and a piece of bread or would you seek the advice of a tournament champion who had won every contest he ever entered?

You would say, "I'll ask the champion!"

If you wanted to be a major league pitcher would you want to be mentored by the greatest pitcher in all of professional baseball or the boy pitching sand lot ball down at the schoolyard?

You would say that you would ask the greatest pitcher of all time!

If you wanted to be a millionaire, would seek the counsel of a man who has made his first million and more or would you ask for financial advice from the man that has never had even two nickels to rub together?

Why of course Brother Charlie I would ask the rich guy!

Well then, let me throw out a novel idea to you. How about if you really want to live a dynamic and fruitful life in Christ, you go find some folks to fellowship with that seem to love Christ more than you do – people that have been walking out their Salvation for years and can give you advise based on their experience concerning what it takes to sustain that relationship in a "LOST WORLD."

Ask them about <u>THEIR</u> Bible reading and Bible study habits and how that has affected <u>THEIR</u> life. Ask them about <u>THEIR</u> daily prayer life and what that has done for <u>THEM</u>. Ask them to share with you some of the miraculous things that Christ has done for them and their families because of their faithfulness. Hanging around folks like <u>THAT</u> every day will encourage you to press on and press in when the trials of life come – and they will.

Fifth: Serve God daily through your service to your fellow man.

[12] My command is this: Love each other as I have loved you. [13] Greater love has no one than this: than to lay down one's life for one's friends.
John 15:12-13 (NIV)

I spent fifty years of my life waking up every morning and spending the rest of my day thinking about what I could do to satisfy MY NEEDS. I was a miserable man, husband, father and friend. I have spent the last twenty years of my life {since I have come to "truly know" Christ} waking up every morning and spending the rest of my day thinking about what I can do to meet SOMEBODY ELSE'S NEEDS. I feel like one of the most blessed men, husbands, fathers and friends walking this planet.

Jesus Christ was the Son of God but all He ever wanted to be was a SERVANT.

5 In your relationships with one another have the same mindset as Christ Jesus:
6 Who, being in very nature God,
did not consider equality with God something to be used to his own advantage;
7 rather, he made himself nothing
by taking the very nature of a servant,
being made in human likeness.
Philippians 2:5-7

If you want to truly be an effective Christian, I highly recommend you assume the role of "lifetime servant" to God and man. It's like spending the day – every day – playing the "YOUR NEXT GAME."

You have <u>GOT</u> to try this Game! <u>Check this out!</u>

You go to a REAL busy store {the busier the better} like a Wal-Mart. You get everything you need in your cart and you and you go up front. But when you get up there {and this is important} you get in the <u>longest line</u> at the checkouts. Yes there are check outs with no one waiting you could get in but you are a servant and you want to play the "YOUR NEXT GAME."

Okay, you're off to a great start. You've picked one with at least six people ahead of you – all of them with their buggies slam full – some of them with screaming kids in their buggies and – Oh! Look! They're training a new cahier on that register and she hasn't got a clue what she's doing. Perfect!

Now this is really the only hard part of the game but it's the part that gets you ready for the "fun" part. You see right now {as a servant in training} you are going to have to <u>learn to be patient</u> until the six people in front of you get checked out and it becomes YOUR TURN.

Hallelujah! The last person in front of you checks out. You can see they are about to get their receipt and leave and "YOUR NEXT." Do you hurriedly reach into your buggy and begin to throw your stuff on the conveyer belt to begin the checkout process?

<u>NO!!!</u> You turn and look behind you where at least ten more people have lined up to check out since you got up there. You smile warmly at the person directly behind you with a rowdy kid in her basket along with a ton of merchandise and you say:

WAIT FOR IT...

"Ma'am would you like to go on ahead? I'm not in a hurry."

She smiles warmly back at you and says, "Thank you SO much, I really appreciate it!" and moves forward.

And you say to yourself, "Man that REALLY made me feel good." And then you suddenly realize –

WOW!!! I'M <u>STILL</u> NEXT

And you know what else is really great? You can stand in that line as long as you want to and let as many people as you want to go ahead of you BUT you will still always be NEXT.

<u>Then</u> - if you decide to let everybody go ahead of you until you are finally the last person in line - guess what happens then.

YOU BECOME FIRST IN LINE!

Is having a Servant's Heart Great or What?

³³ When Christ was in the house, he asked them, "What were you arguing about on the road?"
³⁴ But they kept quiet because on the way they had argued about who was the greatest.
³⁵ Sitting down, Jesus called the Twelve and said, "Anyone who wants to be first must be the very last, and the servant of all."
Mark 9:33-35 (NIV)

STEP 7

OK! YOU HEARD ABOUT HIM!
YOU FOUND OUT ABOUT HIM!
YOU HAVE BEEN SEEKING HIM!
YOU HAVE MET HIM!
YOU HAVE ACCEPTED HIM!
YOU HAVE GOTTEN TO KNOW HIM!
Now the next step:
TRUSTING HIM!

Webster's Definition of the word TRUST - It implies instinctive unquestioning belief in and reliance upon someone or something.

> *5 Trust in the LORD with all your heart and lean not on your own understanding;*
> **Proverbs 3:5 (NIV)**

In order to have lasting value and importance, "Trust" has to be EARNED.

Trust is earned when through close and consistent exposure to someone, they can prove to you unquestionably that they are patently honest in what they say – principled in everything they do – always dependable in what they promise – walking the way they talk - and finally – DEEPLY REPENTANT when they fail you in any of those areas.

I have hundreds of people I know on Social Media and there are hundreds more I have met and fellowshipped with over my life in the private sector and in the Ministry but outside my immediate family there are only a handful of men and women I truly trust and confide in. But even in that group of people we occasionally let each other down.

I have ONE FRIEND and ONE FRIEND ONLY who has NEVER lied to me – NEVER misled me – NEVER turned his back on me – NEVER let me down and NEVER failed to do what he promised me – and His name is JESUS CHRIST.

I want to share some of the words of one of my favorite gospel songs with you called: "If That Isn't Love".

He left the Splendor of Heaven knowing His Destiny
It was the lonely Hill of Golgotha to lay down his life for <u>me</u>
And if that isn't Love then the ocean is dry
There's no stars in the sky and an Eagle can't fly.

When a man sets out to earn MY LOVE by laying down his life for me as described in the words above He has also gained my full TRUST. And my friends He was just getting started.

You see, when I found myself hopelessly lost – caught up in a life of addiction to alcohol, amphetamines, pornography, lying, manipulating and MUCH MORE- I could not find <u>MY</u> way out. And then the voice of Christ spoke to me through those "words in red" in John 14:6 when He said, ***"<u>I</u> AM THE WAY"***

Because I had reached the place by working through the first six steps where I felt I "truly knew Him" - I was now able to TRUST Christ Jesus UNCONDITIONALLY. I was ready to understand and believe that I COULD be free from my past if I would confess the answer that: "It can't be <u>my way</u> and it must be HIS WAY." So now open and ready to trust HIS advice and counsel – He gave me this advice:

5 Put to death, therefore, whatever belongs to your earthly nature: sexual immorality, impurity, lust, evil desires and greed, which is idolatry. 6 Because of these, the wrath of God is coming. 7 You used to walk in these ways, in the life you once lived. 8 But now you must also rid yourselves of all such things as these: anger, rage, malice, slander, and filthy language from your lips. 9 Do not lie to each other, since you have taken off your old self with its practices 10 and have put on the new self, which is being renewed in knowledge in the image of its Creator.
Colossians 3:5-10 (NIV)

When all my "so called friends" {caught up in many of the same behaviors I was} kept heaping the <u>LIES</u> on me that no matter how hard I tried, I would NEVER be any different – LIES like "once an alcoholic always an alcoholic' – "once a druggie always a druggie" and "once a pervert always a pervert" - I fully TRUSTED the voice of Christ who spoke to me again through those "words in red" in John 14:6 when He said, *"<u>I</u> AM THE TRUTH"*

There is an old saying I used to hear a lot when I was younger: "Don't believe <u>anything</u> you hear and <u>only half</u> of what you see." That was long before the internet, dozens of competing news channels, social media and the rampant misinformation we are bombarded by every day from all of them.

There are so many ways now to edit video and audio footage and "doctor" photographs to create what looks real but is anything but, that sadly we have come to the place in our society where that old saying needs to be changed to: "Don't believe <u>anything</u> you hear AND don't believe <u>anything you see either</u>."

I have found one uncompromised source of REAL TRUTH left that I can TRUST if I am the least bit confused about my life and the direction it is going and that source is the Eternal Truth of God's Word.

When a choice comes before me in life and I am not sure what I need to do about it, I don't pick up the phone and call Aunt Sally or Uncle Billy or my next door neighbor or the guy working in the cubicle next me at work – NOPE – I turn to the Holy Spirit inspired inerrant truth given me in my Bible. And trust me when I tell you that when I seek the answers I need in the Word there is always a clear answer there – and I know that I know that it is the truth.

The sad reality is that the world has become comfortable living with and negotiating their way through the lies that the "father of lies" promotes on this earth DAILY. Christ tells us in the book of John that <u>we don't want to hear the truth</u> and WHY.

⁴² Jesus said to them, "If God were your Father, you would love me, for I have come here from God. I have not come on my own; God sent me. ⁴³ Why is my language not clear to you? Because you are unable to hear what I say. ⁴⁴ You belong to your father, the devil, and you want to carry out your father's desires.

He was a murderer from the beginning, not holding to the truth, for there is no truth in him. When he lies, he speaks his native language, for he is a liar and the father of lies. ⁴⁵ Yet because I tell the truth, you do not believe me!

John 8:42-45 (NIV)

There are two important things I had to learn about the TRUTH.

THE TRUTH HURTS!

BUT...

³¹ To those who had believed him, Jesus said, "If you hold to my teaching, you are really my disciples. ³² Then you will know the truth, <u>and the truth will set you free."</u>

John 8:31-32 (NIV)

When in a moment of desperation and despair I found myself on my knees saying: I can't live MY life another day in this condition, He comforted me once more with those "words in red" in John 14:6 when He said, *"I AM THE LIFE"*

6 You see, at just the right time, when we were still powerless, Christ laid down His Life for the ungodly. 7 Very rarely will anyone die for a righteous person, though for a good person someone might possibly dare to die. 8 But God demonstrates his own love for us in this: While we were still sinners, Christ laid down His Life for us.
Romans 5:6-8 (NIV)

Through that selfless sacrifice Christ opened a door that no flesh and blood man could open. He opened the door to the forgiveness of God.

Because Christ was willing to do this to atone for the sins of ALL mankind, God determined that anyone who TRULY received His Son as their personal Lord and Savior and bore the fruit of that relationship "would not perish."

In response to Christ's love for others demonstrated at Calvary, Almighty God resurrected His "one and only Son" from the grave thereby demonstrating His power over Death, Hell and the Grave. Now through that resurrection of Jesus those of us who have received HIM – by living in Him are extended the promise of eternal life.

Christ has taught me that our LIFE HERE ON EARTH is not for SAVING. Life on earth is intended to be TIRELESSLY SPENT, EXHAUSTED and GIVEN AWAY to our fellow man for the Glory of God.

Although the first six steps to "TRULY KNOWING JESUS CHRIST" are all critical to the process, I really feel in my heart that STEP 7 {TRUSTING HIM} became for me the "CORNERSTONE" of my relationship with Him that loosed me into the position to step into my TRUE DESTINY and complete the Works that God placed me on this planet to accomplish.

Webster's definition of the word CORNERSTONE - The chief foundation on which something is constructed or developed: something that is essential or indispensable.

6 For in Scripture it says
See, I lay a stone in Zion,
a chosen and precious cornerstone,
and the one who TRUSTS in Him
will never be put to shame."
1 Peter 2:6 (NIV)

Fully TRUSTING Christ allowed me to move to the next CRITICLY IMPORTANT step in my relationship with Him – a step so important, that if we refuse to take it, we will NEVER bear the fruit of or meet God's definition of "walking out your Salvation." in Christ.

So let's move now to THAT CRITICAL STEP...

STEP 8
OK! YOU HEARD ABOUT HIM!
YOU FOUND OUT ABOUT HIM!
YOU HAVE BEEN SEEKING HIM!
YOU HAVE MET HIM!
YOU HAVE ACCEPTED HIM!
YOU HAVE GOTTEN TO KNOW HIM!
YOU HAVE TRUSTED HIM!
Now the next step:
OBEYING HIM!

Webster's definition of the word OBEDIENCE - to comply with or follow the commands, restrictions, wishes, or instructions of.

[18] *Then Jesus came to them and said, "All authority in heaven and on earth has been given to me.* [19] *Therefore go and make disciples of all nations, baptizing them in the name of the Father and of the Son and of the Holy Spirit,* [20] *and teaching them to obey everything I have commanded you. And surely I am with you always, to the very end of the age."*
Matthew 28:18-20 (NIV)

So, why is it that you and I struggle so hard with life's choices like these?

15 See, I set before you today life and prosperity, death and destruction. 16 For I command you today to love the LORD your God, to walk in <u>obedience</u> to him, and to keep his commands, decrees and laws; then you will live and increase, and the LORD your God will bless you in the land you are entering to possess.
17 But if your heart turns away and you are not <u>obedient</u>, and if you are drawn away to bow down to other gods and worship them, 18 I declare to you this day that you will certainly be destroyed. You will not live long in the land you are crossing the Jordan to enter and possess.
19 This day I call the heavens and the earth as witnesses against you that I have set before you life and death, blessings and curses. Now choose life, so that you and your children may live 20 and that you may love the LORD your God, listen to his voice, and hold fast to him. For the LORD is your life, and he will give you many years in the land he swore to give to your fathers, Abraham, Isaac and Jacob.
Deuteronomy 30:15-20 (NIV)

Why when we are promised <u>blessings</u>, do we choose <u>curses</u>?

And why when we are promised <u>life</u>, do we choose <u>death</u>?

I sincerely believe that the answer lies in the fact that we have chosen to govern our lives by <u>LAW</u> and <u>POLICY</u> and <u>PROCEDURE</u> and <u>RULES</u> and <u>GUIDELINES</u> made by MEN, when in fact, the only way to live a meaningful and productive life is to live by "<u>PRINCIPLE</u>" – in particular, "<u>sound 'Biblical' Principles of Living</u> based on our unshakeable TRUST in Christ."

TRUST IS THE MOTHER OF OBEDIENCE!

Laws, policies, procedures, rules and guidelines are imposed on us by outside authorities who generally are <u>not under our control</u>, <u>do not seek our advice</u> and <u>do not give us a voice</u> in their decisions – but more importantly that <u>WE DO NOT TRUST</u>. This imposition almost always leads to the same reactions in all of us – <u>opposition</u>, <u>opinion</u>, <u>argument</u>, <u>debate</u>, <u>disagreement</u> and <u>OUTRIGHT REBELLION</u>! Many of us have made dangerous, dishonest and destructive choices in our life for no other reason than proving that no outside force or authority can or will control our life.

Living by "<u>SOUND BIBLICAL PRINCIPLES</u>", on the other hand, involves living by "<u>self-imposed</u>" thoughts and ideas and experiences that have stood the test of time as they relate to quality choices concerning life, liberty and the pursuit of happiness - not only in our own lives but in our relationships with others as well.

Living by Biblical Principles, in great contrast to living by law, creates morality, truthfulness, sound judgment, loyalty, fidelity, and commitment, faithfulness, and covenant agreement.

There is probably no one within the sound of my voice who has not said at some point in your life: "It's not about this or that; it's about the 'PRINCIPLE' of the matter." Even thieves have principles. Have you ever heard of the old saying: "There is honor among thieves?" Even prison inmates have principles. Haven't you heard it said that inmates don't "snitch" or "roll over" on their fellow inmates or "partners in crime?"

If "PRINCIPLES" seem important even to the ungodly, how much more important, then, should they be to those of us who want to live a Righteous Life in Christ?

God's Word is loaded from Genesis 1 to the end of Revelation with the most incredibly useful, awesomely powerful, time tested, life changing "principles of living" known to man. To choose to study His word, to allow it to reveal its power to you, to believe it and receive it and to OBEY IT will bring blessings into your life and relationships beyond your imagination.

WHY? – Because the Biblical principles are IN YOU, Christ is IN YOU and the Holy Spirit is IN YOU.

ALL TOGETHER NOW...
When we walk with the Lord
In the light of His Word,
What a glory He sheds on our way;
While we do His good will,
He abides with us still,
And with all who will trust and obey.

Doing what we are told to do according to man's law and man's authority when we don't trust or agree with it is called COMPLIANCE!

Trusting in what we are told to do according to the sound Biblical Teachings found in God's Word because we LOVE Him is OBEDIENCE!

AND OBEDIENCE IS THE MOTHER OF SERVANTHOOD.

So let's move quickly to the next step...

STEP 9

OK! YOU HEARD ABOUT HIM!
YOU FOUND OUT ABOUT HIM!
YOU HAVE BEEN SEEKING HIM!
YOU HAVE MET HIM!
YOU HAVE ACCEPTED HIM!
YOU HAVE GOTTEN TO KNOW HIM!
YOU HAVE TRUSTED HIM!
YOU HAVE OBEYED HIM!
Now the next step:

SUBMITTING TO HIM!

*[6] in all your ways submit to him,
and he will make your paths straight*
Proverbs 3:6 (NIV)

**Webster's definition of the word
SUBMIT - to give over or yield to the
power or authority of another.**

Once you come to the place in your journey where you are beginning to "truly know" Christ, you will have discovered that He will never be satisfied for you to settle for just being a <u>church member</u>. To the contrary – He's <u>not</u> looking for members – He is looking for SERVANTS.

26 *...whoever wants to become great among you must be your servant,* 27 *and whoever wants to be first must be your slave –* 28 *just as the Son of Man did not come to be served, but to serve, and to give his life as a ransom for many."*
Matthew 20:26-28 (NIV)

Let me share a revelation God showed me during a Bible reading that demonstrates the difference in thinking between SERVANTS OF CHRIST and ordinary men.

In Matthew 25 starting in about Verse 31 we are told that in the last days when Jesus comes in all his glory, He will gather ALL THE NATIONS on earth before Him and He will separate them one from another as a shepherd separates the Sheep from the Goats – the Sheep on His Right and the Goats on his left.

³⁴ "Then the King will say to those on his right, 'Come, you who are blessed by my Father; take your inheritance, the kingdom prepared for you since the creation of the world. ³⁵ For I was hungry and you gave me something to eat, I was thirsty and you gave me something to drink, I was a stranger and you invited me in, ³⁶ I needed clothes and you clothed me, I was sick and you looked after me, I was in prison and you came to visit me.'

³⁷ "Then the righteous will answer him, 'Lord, when did we <u>see</u> <u>you</u> hungry and feed you, or thirsty and give you something to drink? ³⁸ When did we <u>see you</u> a stranger and invite you in, or needing clothes and clothe you? ³⁹ When did we <u>see</u> <u>you</u> sick or in prison and go to visit you?'

⁴⁰ "The King will reply, 'Truly I tell you, whatever you did for one of the least of these brothers and sisters of mine, you did for me.'

⁴¹ "Then he will say to those on his left, 'Depart from me, you who are cursed, into the eternal fire prepared for the devil and his angels. ⁴² For I was hungry and you gave me nothing to eat, I was thirsty and you gave me nothing to drink, ⁴³ I was a stranger and you did not invite me in, I needed clothes and you did not clothe me, I was sick and in prison and you did not look after me.'

44 *"They also will answer, 'Lord, when did we <u>see</u> <u>you</u> hungry or thirsty or a stranger or needing clothes or sick or in prison, and did not help you?'* 45 *"He will reply, 'Truly I tell you, whatever you did not do for one of the least of these, you did not do for me.'* 46 *"Then they will go away to eternal punishment, but the righteous to eternal life."*
Matthew 25:34-46 (NIV)

The first time I read these scriptures the Holy Spirit asked me a question that I really didn't know the answer to. The question was: "Charlie Haynes did you notice in these scriptures that BOTH the people Christ considered the Sheep {those who HAD HELPED everyone they found in need} and the people He considered the Goats {those who HAD NOT helped anyone they found in need} responded to Him exactly the same way?"

I answered: "I'm not sure Lord."

So He explained further, "They both said: 'Lord, when did we **see you** hungry and feed you, or thirsty and give you something to drink? When did we **see you** a stranger and invite you in, or needing clothes and clothe you? When did we **see you** sick or in prison and go to visit you?'"

Then the Spirit said, "Charlie, the first thing I want you to recognize is the power of the phrase '**SEE YOU**' repeated in their replies."

Men or women who have a Servant's Heart {the Heart of Christ} '**SEE**' - the Hungry, the Thirsty, the Needy, the Sick and the Outcasts of Society and they are immediately drawn to minister to their need. It comes naturally to a Servant of God. They're not doing it to make points with anyone. They are not keeping a record of how many people they help. They just do it! THAT'S WHY they answered Christ by saying: "When did we do that Lord?"

On the other hand, the man or woman without a servant's heart {and there a WAY more Goats than there are Sheep in this world} not only **do not see** the people all around them in despair – they DON'T WANT TO SEE THEM. They are perfectly happy to go about their way everyday with their "blinders" firmly in place. After all, hunger and homelessness and disease and rape and murder and prejudice and hatred is not on them – that's **those** peoples problem. So in the above Scriptures Christ had to call to **their attention** how useless they were to the Kingdom of God.

When Jesus Christ was on this earth, He did everything in His Power up to and including being openly disrespected, cursed, beaten, tortured and crucified to care for His fellow man – those He refers to lovingly in the scriptures as his Brothers and Sisters.

Now seated firmly at the right hand of the Father in Heaven interceding for you and I against the accusations of Satan until He returns, He fully expects you and I {in the Power of the Holy Spirit He has placed in us} to "get His back" concerning helping each other AND our fellow man. If you call yourself a Christian and settle for anything less – I suggest to you that YOU AIN'T "walking out your salvation with fear and trembling" RIGHT.

REMEMBER!

'Truly I tell you, whatever you did for one of the least of these brothers and sisters of mine, you did for me.'
Matthew 25:40

If Christ paid a drop in visit to earth tomorrow, I can guarantee you He <u>WOULD NOT</u> be hanging out with the "religious folks." He would be hanging out with the "broken folks."

Want Proof? Consider this…

15 While Jesus was having dinner at Levi's house, many tax collectors and sinners were eating with him and his disciples, for there were many who followed him. 16 When the teachers of the law who were Pharisees saw him eating with the sinners and tax collectors, they asked his disciples: "Why does he eat with tax collectors and sinners?"
17 On hearing this, Jesus said to them, "It is not the healthy who need a doctor, but the sick. I have not come to call the righteous, but sinners."
Mark 2:15-17 (NIV)

And This...

Jesus said to them, "Truly I tell you, the tax collectors and the prostitutes are entering the kingdom of God ahead of you. 32 For John came to you to show you the way of righteousness, and you did not believe him, but the tax collectors and the prostitutes did. And even after you saw this, you did not repent and believe him.
Matthew 21:31-32 (NIV)

Finding the willingness to "truly submit" your life to the service of Christ and bearing the fruit of the Salvation He purchase for you WILL NOT be easy. It is not {as some might think} a "fifty yard dash" it is much more like a "triathlon."

There have been times that, in the emotional realm, I felt like I was walking on hot coals and crawling on broken glass but the wounds healed and there was always a Blessing waiting on the other side. When my wife and I surrendered to Christ's call almost twenty years ago, we surrendered to a ministry that few people have any interest in. We have answered Christ's call to found and operate three very successful Six Month <u>Resident</u> Christ Centered Addiction Recovery Centers – one for women and two for men. By the time these men and women come to us for help they have hit "rock bottom." Many of the women we minister to have been molested, misused, disrespected, beaten, pimped out, enslaved, abandoned and incarcerated. Many have lost custody of their children and ALL have lost all hope.

Many of the men we minister to {although they have work skills} can't hold a job or accumulate any wealth because what they <u>do</u> earn is immediately blown on deepening drug use. Unfortunately, many of these young men have grown up without a reputable "father figure" in their life and are left to be raised and mentored by "life in the streets".

Is it hard to minister to broken men and women who have given up on themselves and their future and believe that "it will never be any different than it is right now?" **YES!!!** Is it worth it? **ABSOLUTELY!!!** And let me tell you **WHY...**

As willing Servants of God, we get to be the first person maybe in years that gets to look into a broken woman's face – wipe the tears from her eyes and promise her it **IS** going to be different.

As the days go by we get to see the first smile come on her face – her first burst of laughter – her first positive interaction with other residents – the morning she comes down from her room standing straighter, shoulders back and a look of confidence on her face that lets you know "she believes she can make it."

The older more experienced men on our staff get to come alongside the younger men in our program and become the mentoring father figures they never had growing up. We get to be there to see the light come on as we teach them about God's plan for their lives as Spirit Leaders of their families. We are there to teach them sound Biblical Principles of Living concerning the duties of a loving and faithful husband and father toward their wives and children that they have not only **NOT** discussed with their natural fathers but in most cases never saw demonstrated either.

We get to see broken families healed and put back together. We get to see men and women regain custody of the children they thought they had lost forever. We get to see marriages saved.

We get to see charges dropped, records expunged and court cases thrown out. We get to lead people to knowing Christ and we get to see them follow in the waters of Baptism. EVERY DAY we get to see God at work in broken lives. What a life!

When all you have **EVER** known growing up around in your family or your surroundings is complete chaos {as bad as it seems} you can begin to think it's "normal." Thanks be to Christ, we get a chance to show them that it's not.

So what does it take to be submitted to Christ deep enough and wide enough for Him to look at you – smile – and say: "Well done my good and faithful Servant." I stumbled across this great answer to that question in an article {author unknown} on a website called: www.heprayed.com.

READ IT! RECEIVE IT! LIVE BY IT!

The Heart of a Servant

If you want to be like Jesus, you have to be a servant with a good heart. He said, "I came to serve, not to be served." (Mat 20:28). Below are the characteristics of a true servant of God.

- A true servant of God will be willing to serve in lowly areas – areas that nobody else would want to serve in. These are areas where there is no recognition from other people. They are areas where much work is done behind the scenes and others don't even consider the fact that it needed to be done!

- The true servant of God is willing to do this because he or she is working before the Lord, not before men. This is not only done at church or in the "body", but especially at home! Stephen was the first Christian martyr. His story is in Acts and of him the bible says that he was 'filled with the Spirit.' (Acts 6:5). They chose this Spirit filled man to do a very lowly task – take care of old women who could not take care of themselves. This godly man was willing to work a tedious job at the nursing home for God and he didn't complain even once!

- The next characteristic of a true servant of God is that this person gives and serves without expecting anything in return. In 2 Corinthians 12:15 Paul pointed out to those people "the more I love you, the less I'm loved by you." Yet he was still willing to spend and be spent for them! That's godliness; loving people unconditionally and doing good to them without expecting anything back – not even love or appreciation.

- This next level of servitude I've found to be the most difficult. The true servant of God will be willing to give of his or herself even to their enemies. By "enemies", I don't just mean people who want to avoid you all the time and never talk to you. Your enemy could be your spouse or a friend who is in a bad mood at the time, and treats you harshly. It could be your teenage child who wants nothing to do with you at the time. They are not really your enemies – but maybe for the time being, they are acting like you're an enemy! During these times, the true servant of God will really stand out.

It takes a godly person to do good to another even when that other person is treating them like trash in return. Jesus said that we must love people even especially at these times, otherwise we're just the same as the world (who only love people that treat them nicely) (Mat 5:43-47).

- A true servant will never boast, or think of himself highly because he is serving the Lord. It won't even enter his mind that he did such good deeds! In other words, his "left hand will not know what his right hand is doing" (Mat 6:3). His attitude will be, "I'm just doing my job."

- Lastly, true servants of God will serve with joy all these times as if they are serving the Lord. They will never complain that they've been given such a lowly task. These people realize that anything they do for others, it is like they're doing it for their Lord (Mat 25:40), and they will rejoice at that fact that they have the privilege to serve God like that.

Now that you have reached that important step in your walk where you are truly submitted to and in the full service of Christ as His loving and faithful servant you are ready for the next step.

SO, Let's Go!

STEP 10

OK! YOU HEARD ABOUT HIM!
YOU FOUND OUT ABOUT HIM!
YOU HAVE BEEN SEEKING HIM!
YOU HAVE MET HIM!
YOU HAVE ACCEPTED HIM!
YOU HAVE GOTTEN TO KNOW HIM!
YOU HAVE TRUSTED HIM!
YOU HAVE OBEYED HIM!
YOU HAVE SUBMITTED TO HIM!
Now the next step:

LIVING FOR HIM!

*[4] The word of the LORD came to me, saying,
[5] "Before I formed you in the womb I knew you,
before you were born I set you apart; I appointed
you as a prophet to the nations."*
Jeremiah 1:4-5 (NIV)

When we turn on our television, pick up a newspaper, or scan the internet – we shake our heads is in despair and disgust and complain to the person sitting alongside us, "What in the world is wrong with our country" and "What is it coming to?"

I believe that what is wrong with the United States of America, including ANY State, County, City, Township or Cross Road Community in this once great nation called America is <u>NOT</u> the fault of the President, <u>NOT</u> the fault of the Congress, <u>NOT</u> the fault of the Senate, and <u>NOT</u> the fault of the Supreme Court.

The truth is that an ever increasing "moral decay" of this once great and noble nation has brought on rampant hatred and bigotry and prejudice and lying and anger and greed and selfishness and murder and rape and robbery AND the ever increasing destruction of the American family at ALL levels of our society.

It breaks my heart to say that this terrible dilemma that we have found ourselves in must be laid directly at the feet of those of us who openly state and profess that we are Christians BUT live our lives in desperation, defeat and hopelessness...

I'm talking about those of us who know all the "religious" things to say around our "religious" friends but wouldn't dare to bring up Christ's name in a crowd if we thought it might offend somebody.

In particular, I'm talking about those of us who are so quick to broadcast that "Christ died for us" but in truth won't spend an hour of our time "<u>living for Him</u>."

By the time we get to this step in our journey to "Truly Knowing Jesus" we should have figured out that there is WAY MORE to "walking out our salvation" through a right relationship with Christ than going to a church every once in a while - then singing a few hymns – listening to a twenty minute sermon – shouting AMEN and heading to the house.

Living for Christ is about passion. It's about faithfulness. It's about devotion. It's about sacrifice. It's about service. It's about obedience. It's about a twenty four hour a day – seven day a week crusade against the things of Hell for the Glory of God.

It's not about what you think you can or cannot accomplish – It's all about what He knows He can accomplish THROUGH YOU if you will "live for Him."

It's about you understanding and coming into agreement with the truth that you are SPECIAL and set aside by God Almighty to accomplish those things on this earth that He created you to accomplish.

Please take a minute and study the following scripture with me. I know of no other group of scriptures in God's Word that paint a more beautiful picture of just how intimate his relationship with us is.

> *¹ You have searched me, LORD,*
> *and you know me.*

There is no one on this earth that KNOWS more about you or CARES more about you than Jesus Christ - <u>not even **YOU**</u>. And the amazing thing is that He loves you **IN SPITE** of what He knows – unlike your "so called friends."

> *² You know when I sit and when I rise;*
> *you perceive my thoughts from afar.*
> *³ You discern my going out and my lying down;*
> *you are familiar with <u>all my ways.</u>*

Yes, He is completely aware of how you often have a way of lying or stealing or manipulating or cheating or exaggerating or not keeping your word or gossiping about your friends or lacing your conversation with an overabundance of profanity.

But guess what? He still loves you and is patiently waiting for you to finally make the decision to give all that up to "live for Him."

⁴ Before a word is on my tongue
you, LORD, know it completely.

I remember back in BC {before Christ} that I had gotten to a point in my life where honestly I don't think I could complete a full sentence without having at least one cuss word thrown in there somewhere. As a matter of fact, I think I thought the more of them I could squeeze in there, the better the sentence was. After all, how can you get your point across without throwing a few cuss words in? And how could I hold up my reputation for knowing more dirty jokes that anybody in my circle of "friends" if I didn't have a truck load of good cuss words ready to make the jokes even funnier?

Well obviously when I determined I was going to begin to "live for Christ" I knew that kind of language would NOT line up with what He expected of me.

Then I remembered the verse in Psalms 139:4 {above} and I said: LORD! You said in your Word that before a word is on my tongue – you know it – so I am asking you Lord, the next time anything profane or unpleasing to you STARTS to come out of my mouth – STOP IT!

You have every right to believe or not believe what I am telling you; but, He REMOVED profanity out of my mind and heart. He has also shown me over and over in these last twenty years while standing in the Pulpit every Sunday morning – that I can indeed make a point very strongly and very plainly to those listening WITHOUT using profanity. Awe, come on Brother Charlie, You mean to tell me in twenty years you have never dropped even one "F Bomb"? Well yes I do have this one "F Bomb" God lets me drop when I preach and I do. That F Bomb is…FREEDOM!!!!!!!

5 You hem me in behind and before,
and you lay your hand upon me.
6 Such knowledge is too wonderful for me,
too lofty for me to attain.

7 Where can I go from your Spirit?
Where can I flee from your presence?
8 If I go up to the heavens, you are there;
if I make my bed in Hell, you are there.

I have made my bed in Hell MANY times in my life. The truth is, by the world's standards I should be either an outcast, diseased, imprisoned or dead for the ignorant, sick, stupid and depraved things I have done in my life. I didn't know then that even in the depths of my sin, God had his hand of protection on me. He knew what I could not have known, that the day would come that I would turn away from those things and turn to His Son for the redemption of those sins and that I would indeed determine to live the rest of my life for that Son – Christ Jesus.

Have you been fluffing your pillows in Hell? It's not too late to turn.

⁹ If I rise on the wings of the dawn,
if I settle on the far side of the sea,
¹⁰ even there your hand will guide me,
your right hand will hold me fast.
¹¹ If I say, "Surely the darkness will hide me
and the light become night around me,"
¹² even the darkness will not be dark to you;
the night will shine like the day,
for darkness is as light to you.

When I look back over my life I remember that most all the sinful things I did were done in the "DARK." Isn't it amazing to realize that by hiding our sin behind closed doors and pulled curtains and dark places that we think we are "getting away with it"?

Oh! Sure, your mother or your dad or your children or your neighbor or your boss or whoever might never know. BUT wait till your growing love for and submission to Christ causes a Spiritual brain cell to kick in, like it did with me, and you realize that in those dark sinful moments, the night shines like day to God and that same sinful darkness was as light to Him.

He was watching my every single sin unfold – every single time – and yet He forgave me for Christ's sake and has used me as His chosen instrument.

> *¹³ For you created my inmost being;*
> *you knit me together in my mother's womb.*
> *¹⁴ I praise you because I am fearfully and*
> *wonderfully made;*
> *your works are wonderful,*
> *I know that full well.*
> *¹⁵ My frame was not hidden from you*
> *when I was made in the secret place,*
> *when I was woven together in the depths of the*
> *earth.*
> *¹⁶ Your eyes saw my unformed body;*
> *all the days ordained for me were written in your*
> *book*
> *before one of them came to be.*

I believe that "all the days ordained for me" talked about in the above scripture do not include the days of our "sinful life." I believe He is talking about the days of our DESTINY.

The way I explain it to myself and others is that "before we were knit in our mother's womb" there was a blueprint on the table in Heaven concerning God's plan for our life in service to Him. The blue print is and always has been and always will be on the table. The only question remaining is if and when you and I are going to make the decisions to begin to live by that blueprint.

God is patiently waiting for you and I to make up our minds. When we are ready to get started – He will be ready to accommodate.

> [17] *How precious to me are your thoughts, God!*
> *How vast is the sum of them!*
> [18] *Were I to count them,*
> *they would outnumber the grains of sand –*
> *when I awake, I am still with you.*
> **Psalm 139:1-18 (NIV)**

When you know that you know that you know all the steps we have taken so far in this long journey to "TRULY KNOWING" your Lord and Savior, Christ Jesus, are instilled in your Heart, Mind, Soul, and Spirit; you will come to the awesome place where you know and believe – asleep or awake – rich or poor – sick or well – alone or surrounded – happy or sad – HE IS STILL WITH YOU –

Because NOW you have reached the 11th Step

STEP 11

OK! YOU HEARD ABOUT HIM!
YOU FOUND OUT ABOUT HIM!
YOU HAVE BEEN SEEKING HIM!
YOU HAVE MET HIM!
YOU HAVE ACCEPTED HIM!
YOU HAVE GOTTEN TO KNOW HIM!
YOU HAVE TRUSTED HIM!
YOU HAVE OBEYED HIM!
YOU HAVE SUBMITTED TO HIM!
YOU HAVE BEEN LIVING FOR HIM!
Now the next step:

LIVING IN HIM!

8 Therefore, there is now no condemnation for those who are IN Christ Jesus, 2 because through Christ Jesus the law of the Spirit who gives life has set you free from the law of sin and death.
Romans 8:1-2 (NIV)

I can remember asking God at one point in my journey to "truly knowing" my Savior, "Lord how will I know that I know that I have gone from just living <u>FOR</u> Christ to living IN HIM?"

Remember how I have told you that there is NO question you will ever have about how to live your life that is not answered in God's Word. Well, guess where He sent me to get the answer to my question – YEP! "The Word."

¹⁷ *Therefore, if anyone is <u>IN</u> Christ, he is a <u>new creation</u>; the <u>old has gone</u>, the <u>new has come</u>!*
2 Corinthians 5:17 (NIV)

Having read the verse as He instructed, I then said, "OK! Lord, what do you want me to take from this verse?" And <u>this</u> is what He spoke into my Spirit:

"My son this verse contains the ingredients of proof positive that you have matured to the point in your relationship with Christ that you are TRULY living <u>IN</u> Him – the ultimate goal of your Salvation.

Now what I want you to do is go into your bathroom right now and look deeply into the 'Spiritual Mirror of Truth.' What I mean by that, my son, is that you don't look into that mirror as you always have to groom your exterior like combing you hair or trimming your beard. NO, I mean to look into the mirror and for maybe the first time look deep into your own soul – be ready to question yourself in truth – and then ask yourself this, 'Charlie Haynes WHAT IS <u>NEW</u> ABOUT YOU?' Having gone through all the steps you have to get to this point, surely you can find some positive things to say."

So I did as He requested.

I stood in front of the mirror and probably for the first time in my life I ignored my outward appearance and looked deep into my own eyes. It was a weird feeling to be examining my own soul concerning where I had "become NEW" in my relationship with Christ.

But I received some encouragement when I was able to recall a few things that <u>WERE</u> new about me.

I was able to TRUTHFULLY say, "Well Charlie, you didn't lay your head on a pillow at night for twenty years of your life sober, BUT you're not an alcoholic any more. You're not a pill head anymore. You're not a sex addict or pornography addict anymore. You're not lying to your family about where you've been any more. You're not stealing from your employers anymore."

Then I break into a BIG smile at myself in the mirror and shouted,

"WOW! THERE IS A WHOLE LOT THAT"S NEW ABOUT ME, LORD."

Then my smile began to fade when the Voice of God spoke to me again and said, "Wait a minute my son, you have forgotten that there are <u>TWO</u> parts to that scripture that must be examined to assure you that you are living <u>IN</u> Christ.

You have talked about the things that are <u>NEW</u> about you but you must now turn back to the Spiritual Mirror – look deep into your own soul in truth one more time - and ask yourself this question, 'OK! Charlie Haynes, what is still **OLD** about you?'"

When you truthfully KNOW that ALL of the old sinful behaviors that were once in your life have been confessed – repented of and placed at the Foot of the Cross you are crossing the threshold of not only "TRULY KNOWING" Jesus Christ but beginning to LIVE <u>IN</u> HIM as well.

As you continue to walk out your Salvation "<u>IN</u> CHRIST" for the rest of your days on this earth, you will now begin to live your life with a new set of understandings – like THIS ONE:

3 For though we live in the world, we do not wage war as the world does. 4 The weapons we fight with are not the weapons of the world. On the contrary, they have divine power to demolish strongholds. 5 We demolish arguments and every pretension that sets itself up against the knowledge of God, and we take captive every thought to make it obedient to Christ. 6 And we will be ready to punish every act of disobedience, once your obedience is complete.
2 Corinthians 10:3-6 (NIV)

AND THIS WILL BE YOUR ANTHEM...

7 But whatever were {worldly} gains to me I now consider loss for the sake of Christ. 8 What is more, I consider everything a loss because of the surpassing worth of knowing Christ Jesus my Lord, for whose sake I have lost all things. I consider them garbage, that I may gain Christ 9 and be found <u>IN HIM</u>, not having a righteousness of my own that comes from the law, but that which is through faith in Christ — the righteousness that comes from God on the basis of faith.
Philippians 3:7-9 (NIV)

AND THIS WILL BECOME YOUR POSTURE...

¹⁰ Finally, be strong in the Lord and in his mighty power. ¹¹ Put on the full armor of God, so that you can take your stand against the devil's schemes. ¹² For our struggle is not against flesh and blood, but against the rulers, against the authorities, against the powers of this dark world and against the spiritual forces of evil in the heavenly realms. ¹³ Therefore put on the full armor of God, so that when the day of evil comes, you may be able to stand your ground, and after you have done everything, to stand. ¹⁴ <u>Stand firm then</u>, with the belt of truth buckled around your waist, with the breastplate of righteousness in place, ¹⁵ and with your feet fitted with the readiness that comes from the gospel of peace. ¹⁶ In addition to all this, take up the shield of faith, with which you can extinguish all the flaming arrows of the evil one. ¹⁷ Take the helmet of salvation and the sword of the Spirit, which is the word of God.
¹⁸ And pray in the Spirit on all occasions with all kinds of prayers and requests. With this in mind, be alert and always keep on praying for all the Lord's people.
Ephesians 6:10-18 (NIV)

THIS WILL BE YOUR COMPASS...

17 So I tell you this, and insist on it in the Lord, that you must no longer live as the WORLD does, in the futility of their thinking. 18 They are darkened in their understanding and separated from the life of God because of the ignorance that is in them due to the hardening of their hearts. 19 Having lost all sensitivity, they have given themselves over to sensuality so as to indulge in every kind of impurity, and they are full of greed. 20 That, however, is not the way of life you learned 21 when you heard about Christ and were taught in him in accordance with the truth that is in Jesus. 22 You were taught with regard to your former way of life, to put off your old self, which is being corrupted by its deceitful desires; 23 to be made new in the attitude of your minds; 24 and to put on the new self, created to be like God in true righteousness and holiness. 25 Therefore each of you must put off falsehood and speak truthfully to your neighbor, for we are all members of one body. 26 "In your anger do not sin." Do not let the sun go down while you are still angry, 27 and do not give the devil a foothold.

28 Anyone who has been stealing must steal no longer, but must work, doing something useful with their own hands, that they may have something to share with those in need. 29 Do not let any unwholesome talk come out of your mouths, but only what is helpful for building others up according to their needs, that it may benefit those who listen. 30 And do not grieve the Holy Spirit of God, with whom you were sealed for the day of redemption. 31 Get rid of all bitterness, rage and anger, brawling and slander, along with every form of malice. 32 Be kind and compassionate to one another, forgiving each other, just as in Christ God forgave you. 5 1 Follow God's example, therefore, as dearly loved children 2 and walk in the way of love, just as Christ loved us and gave himself up for us as a fragrant offering and sacrifice to God.

3 But among you there must not be even a hint of sexual immorality, or of any kind of impurity, or of greed, because these are improper for God's holy people. 4 Nor should there be obscenity, foolish talk or coarse joking, which are out of place, but rather thanksgiving.

⁵ <u>For of this you can be sure</u>: No immoral, impure or greedy person — such a person is an idolater — has any inheritance in the kingdom of Christ and of God. ⁶ Let no one deceive you with empty words, for because of such things God's wrath comes on those who are disobedient. ⁷ Therefore do not be partners with them.

⁸ For you were once darkness, but now you are light in the Lord. Live as children of light ⁹ (for the fruit of the light consists in all goodness, righteousness and truth) ¹⁰ and find out what pleases the Lord. ¹¹ Have nothing to do with the fruitless deeds of darkness, but rather expose them. ¹² It is shameful even to mention what the disobedient do in secret. ¹³ But everything exposed by the light becomes visible — and everything that is illuminated becomes a light. ¹⁴ This is why it is said:
"Wake up, sleeper,
rise from the dead,
and Christ will shine on you."

¹⁵ Be very careful, then, how you live — not as unwise but as wise, ¹⁶ making the most of every opportunity, because the days are evil. ¹⁷ Therefore do not be foolish, but understand what the Lord's will is.

¹⁸ Do not get drunk on wine, which leads to debauchery. Instead, be filled with the Spirit,

19 speaking to one another with psalms, hymns, and songs from the Spirit. Sing and make music from your heart to the Lord, 20 always giving thanks to God the Father for everything, in the name of our Lord Jesus Christ.

21 Submit to one another out of reverence for Christ. 22 Wives, submit yourselves to your own husbands as you do to the Lord. 23 For the husband is the head of the wife as Christ is the head of the church, his body, of which he is the Savior. 24 Now as the church submits to Christ, so also wives should submit to their husbands in everything.

25 Husbands, love your wives, just as Christ loved the church and gave himself up for her 26 to make her holy, cleansing her by the washing with water through the word, 27 and to present her to himself as a radiant church, without stain or wrinkle or any other blemish, but holy and blameless.

Ephesians 4:17-5:27 (NIV)

AND THIS WILL BE YOUR PRAYER OF THANKSGIVING...

12 I thank Christ Jesus our Lord, who has given me strength, that he considered me trustworthy, appointing me to his service. 13 Even though I was once a blasphemer and a persecutor and a violent man, I was shown mercy because I acted in ignorance and unbelief. 14 The grace of our Lord was poured out on me abundantly, along with the faith and love that are in Christ Jesus.
15 Here is a trustworthy saying that deserves full acceptance: Christ Jesus came into the world to save sinners — of whom I am the worst. 16 But for that very reason I was shown mercy so that in me, the worst of sinners, Christ Jesus might display his immense patience as an example for those who would believe in him and receive eternal life.
1 Timothy 1:12-16 (NIV)

AND NOW THE FINAL STEP TO: "TRULY KNOWING" JESUS CHRIST!"

STEP 12

OK! YOU HEARD ABOUT HIM!
YOU FOUND OUT ABOUT HIM!
YOU HAVE BEEN SEEKING HIM!
YOU HAVE MET HIM!
YOU HAVE ACCEPTED HIM!
YOU HAVE GOTTEN TO KNOW HIM!
YOU HAVE TRUSTED HIM!
YOU HAVE OBEYED HIM!
YOU HAVE SUBMITTED TO HIM!
YOU HAVE BEEN LIVING FOR HIM!
YOU HAVE BEEN LIVING IN HIM!
Now the next and <u>final</u> step:

REIGNING WITH HIM!

[24] *"Father, I want those you have given me to be with me where I am, and to see my glory, the glory you have given me because you loved me before the creation of the world.*
John 17:24 (NIV)

THIS is the <u>Son of God</u> praying for <u>YOU</u> <u>and I,</u> to be allowed to "hang out" with Him FOREVER in the Kingdom of Heaven.

15 He is the image of the invisible God, the firstborn over all creation. 16 For in Him all things were created: things in heaven and on earth, visible and invisible, whether thrones or powers or rulers or authorities; all things have been created through Him and for Him. 17 He is before all things, and in Him all things hold together. 18 And He is the head of the body, the church; He is the beginning and the firstborn from among the dead, so that in everything He might have the supremacy. 19 For God was pleased to have all his fullness dwell in Him, 20 and through Him to reconcile to Himself all things, whether things on earth or things in Heaven, by making peace through His blood, shed on the cross.

21 Once you were alienated from God and were enemies in your minds because of your evil behavior. 22 But now He has reconciled you by Christ's physical body through death to present you holy in his sight, without blemish and free from accusation.

Colossians 1:15-22 (NIV)

The most joyous moment you and I will ever know is that moment when Christ's prayer given in John 17 is answered and we stand before Him in Heaven "face to face" and hear those words that every man and woman who has "TRULY KNOWN" Jesus Christ in Faith and in Spirit while on this earth <u>longs</u> to hear:

"Well done, my good and faithful servant! Come and share your Master's happiness."

We shake our heads in wonderment at the majesty of our New Eternal Home and we say to ourselves – "There is no way I deserve to be here."

Then, you remember back to those days when you were hopelessly lost in your sin and you remember the promises He made you in His Word – Promises like these…

³ At one time you were foolish, disobedient, deceived and enslaved by all kinds of passions and pleasures. You lived in malice and envy, being hated and hating others. ⁴ But when the kindness and love of God our Savior appeared, ⁵ He saved you, not because of righteous things you had done, but because of His mercy. He saved you through the washing of rebirth and renewal by the Holy Spirit, ⁶ whom He poured out on you generously through Jesus Christ our Savior, ⁷ so that, having been justified by His grace, you might become His heir having the hope of eternal life.

Titus 3:3-7 (NIV)

PROMISE MADE - PROMISE KEPT!

²² But now that you have been set free from sin and have become slaves of God, the benefit you reap leads to holiness, and the result is eternal life. ²³ For the wages of sin is death, but the gift of God is eternal life in Christ Jesus our Lord.

Romans 6:22-23 (NIV)

PROMISE MADE – PROMISE KEPT!

⁵ But because of your stubbornness and your unrepentant heart, you stored up wrath against yourself for the day of God's wrath, when His righteous judgment would be revealed. ⁶ God "will repay each person according to what they have done." ⁷ To those who by persistence in doing good sought glory, honor and immortality, <u>He will give eternal life.</u>

Romans 2:5-7 (NIV)

PROMISE MADE - PROMISE KEPT!

²⁵ Jesus answered, "I did tell you, but you did not believe. The works I do in my Father's name testify about me, ²⁶ but you did not believe because you were not my sheep. ²⁷ My sheep listen to my voice; I know them, and they follow me. ²⁸ <u>I give them eternal life</u>, and <u>they shall never perish</u>; <u>no one will snatch them out of my hand.</u>

John 10:25-28 (NIV)

PROMISE MADE - PROMISE KEPT!

35 Then Jesus declared, "I am the bread of life. Whoever comes to me will never go hungry, and whoever believes in me will never be thirsty. 36 But as I told you, you have seen me and still you did not believe. 37 All those the Father gives me will come to me, and whoever comes to me I will never drive away. 38 For I have come down from heaven not to do my will but to do the will of Him who sent me. 39 And this is the will of Him who sent me that I shall lose none of all those He has given me, but raise them up at the last day. 40 For my Father's will is that everyone who looks to the Son and believes in Him shall have <u>eternal life</u>, and I will raise them up at the last day."
John 6:35-40 (NIV)

PROMISE MADE - PROMISE KEPT!

24 "Very truly I tell you, whoever hears my Word and believes Him who sent me <u>has eternal life</u> and will not be judged but has crossed over from death to life. 25 Very truly I tell you, <u>a time is coming and has now come when the dead will hear the voice of the Son of God and those who hear will live.</u>
John 5:24-25 (NIV)

PROMISE MADE - PROMISE KEPT!

Let me close with this. In my twenty years in the ministry I have been present in homes and hospital rooms where death was eminent in a person's life. One of the most beautiful and encouraging things I have been witness to is the death of a man or woman who have NO DOUBT in their mind about where they stand in their relationship with Jesus Christ.

In faith they have spent their latter years walking out those steps I have talked about in this book and there is PEACE that comes over them when they take those final breaths that leaves others speechless. Equally inspiring is being able to witness the peace in the hearts of their family as they as they see their loved one pass from this world. They have the assurance of that loved ones Spiritual Destiny and the Faith to believe that if they continue to walk out THEIR Salvation with "fear and trembling" – they will see their love one again in Heaven.

When I lay my head down on my pillow each night, I shake my head in wonderment concerning the miraculous transformation that has taken place in my life since I started that step by step journey to "Truly Knowing" Christ.

I prayerfully thank Him for loving me in spite of my sins against Him and for the path to redemption He revealed to me through the Power of His Word. I find great comfort in already knowing that as I lay somewhere – someday - drawing MY last breath on earth, that I will join the ranks of those I have seen go in peace and that MY family will REJOICE at my passing because they also know MY Spiritual Destiny.

BE BLESSED!